YI SANG: SELECTED WORKS

Yi Sang

SELECTED WORKS

EDITED BY DON MEE CHOI

TRANSLATED BY JACK JUNG, SAWAKO NAKAYASU,

DON MEE CHOI, AND JOYELLE MCSWEENEY

WAVE BOOKS SEATTLE AND NEW YORK

Published by Wave Books

www.wavepoetry.com

Wave Books titles are distributed to the trade by

Consortium Book Sales and Distribution

Phone: 800-283-3572 / SAN 631-760X

Library of Congress Cataloging-in-Publication Data

Names: Sang, Yi, 1910–1937, author. | Choi, Don Mee, editor, translator. |
    Jung, Jack (Jack Saebyok), translator. | Nakayasu, Sawako, 1975–
    translator. | McSweeney, Joyelle, 1976– translator.

Title: Yi Sang : selected works / edited by Don Mee Choi ; translated by
    Jack Jung, Sawako Nakayasu, Don Mee Choi, and Joyelle McSweeney.

Description: First edition. | Seattle : Wave Books, 2020.

Identifiers: LCCN 2020015634 | ISBN 9781950268085 (paperback)

Subjects: LCSH: Sang, Yi, 1910–1937—Translations into English.

Classification: LCC PL991.9.S3 A2 2020 | DDC 895.73/3—dc23

LC record available at https://lccn.loc.gov/2020015634

Designed by Crisis

Printed in the United States of America

9 8 7 6 5 4 3 2

Yi Sang: Selected Works is published under the support
of Literature Translation Institute of Korea (LTI Korea).

LTI Korea
Literature Translation Institute of Korea

Contents

POEMS

translated from the Korean by Jack Jung

〔

CROW'S EYE VIEW

IV

PARADISE LOST

POEMS

translated from the Japanese by Sawako Nakayasu

INTRODUCTION TO THE JAPANESE POEMS OF YI SANG

FROM **ABNORMAL REVERSIBLE REACTION**

STORIES

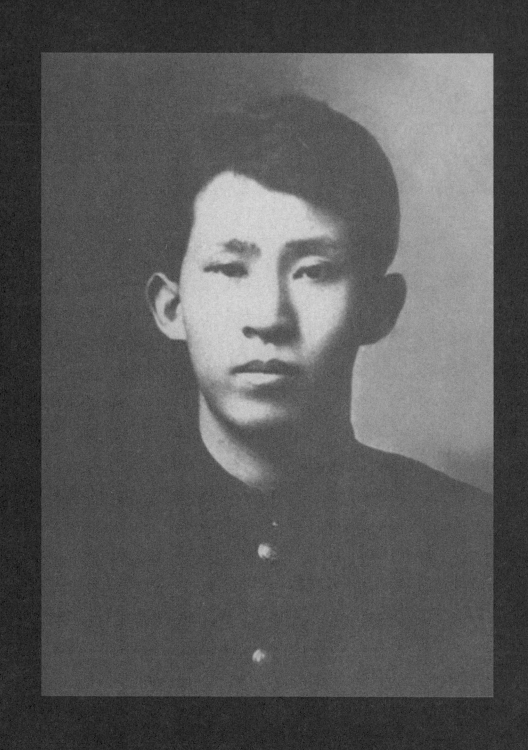

YI SANG: A TIMELINE

JACK JUNG

1910 August 29, Japan-Korea Annexation was signed, making Korea a protectorate of Japan, and the Korean emperor conceded sovereignty of the Korean territory to the Emperor of Japan, effectively establishing Japanese hegemony over the Korean peninsula.

Born September 23, Yi Sang was the eldest of three children, having one sister and one brother. His given name was Kim Hye-kyŏng. Yi Sang was his pen name that he chose later in life. Yi Sang's father, Kim Yŏng-ch'ang, worked in the printing office of the Royal Palace of Korea just before the beginning of the imperial Japanese period. In an accident at the printing office, Yi Sang's father lost his fingers and had to quit his job. Afterwards, he opened a barbershop to support his family. In his essay "A Journey into the Mountain Village," Yi Sang conjures the sound of scissors while recalling his childhood.

1913 Yi Sang was "adopted" by his uncle Kim Yŏn-p'il, his father's older brother, and was raised in his uncle's household. His uncle, the eldest male sibling in his generation of the Kim family, could not produce a male heir with his wife. This made Yi Sang the eldest male child in the family, and the traditional inheritor of a family's name and mantle of responsibility. Yi Sang became a surrogate son of his uncle, and his uncle financially supported his education.

1914 Around this time in Zürich, Switzerland, a group of artists, poets, and writers began an avant-garde literary movement now collectively known as Dadaism. Dadaists' experimentalism, especially that of typographical literary innovations, became an important source of inspiration for Yi Sang's poetry in the colonial Korea of the 1930s.

1919 March 1, a massive nonviolent protest broke out throughout the Korean peninsula against the repressive colonial rule of the Japanese Empire. The event began with the reading of the formal Korean Declaration of Independence. The declaration was made in conjunction with announcement of several complaints against the Japanese governor-general. The complaints addressed issues of discrimination made by the government when employing Koreans versus Japanese people, a disparity in the quality of education being offered to Korean and Japanese people, mistreatment and open disregard of Koreans by the Japanese occupiers, heavy taxes, forced labor, land confiscation, suppression of Korean culture and teachings at schools, and exploitation of Korean labor and resources. The declaration and the protests that followed, which involved nearly two million Koreans participating in over 1,500 demonstrations, were brutally put down by the Japanese police force and military, and several thousands were massacred.

1922 During high school, Yi Sang aspired to become an artist. His education up to this point, and even beyond, would have entirely been taught by Japanese instructors, and almost all of his studies done in Japanese.

1924 André Breton's "Surrealist Manifesto" was published. Yi Sang did not directly reference Breton's manifesto in his writing, but the influence of surrealism, along with that of surrealism's predecessor Dadaism, are crucial aspects of his work.

1925 In August, Korea Artista Proleta Federacio was formed. More popularly known as KAPF, these Korean socialist artists used Esperanto to write their organization's name in international solidarity with the proletariats of the world. The KAPF members were involved in fierce debates on the societal role of art in the colonial era and created radical works of poetry and fiction. They were Yi Sang's contemporaries and a major presence in the Korean literary scene when he began to publish his own writing. Yi Sang's poetry and prose have been categorized as Korean modernist writings by Korean literary scholars since his death. In fact, Yi Sang's work would be considered as having introduced key modes and concepts of Dada and surrealism into Korean literature. Like the artists of KAPF, Yi Sang engaged the critical issues of his day with his own radically experimental poetics.

1926 After graduation, Yi Sang attended a vocational school to become an architect.

1928 In a yearbook of his vocational school, Yi Sang first signed his name as "Yi Sang" rather than using his given name, Kim Hye-kyŏng. Professor Kwŏn Yŏng-min of Seoul National University has proposed a theory that Yi Sang came up with his pen name in order to honor a gift given to him by a fellow painter friend at the same school. The gift was purportedly a painter's box made out of plum wood. The Literary Chinese characters for Yi Sang's name are 李箱. The first character, 李 (Yi), means "plum tree," and the second character, 箱 (Sang), means "box." Yi Sang's painter friend was likely Korean impressionist painter Gu Bon-woong (1906–1953), who was Yi Sang's schoolmate. Later, Gu Bon-woong would also paint a portrait of Yi Sang, titled "Portrait of a Friend."

1929 After graduating first in his class, Yi Sang was appointed as an architect for the governor-general of Korea. Yi Sang also became a member of the Society of Chosun Architects, which was founded by Japanese architects living in Korea in

1922. He entered a competition for the cover design of the society's academic journal, *Chosun and Architecture* (朝鮮と建築), and won the competition in both first and third place.

1930 Yi Sang published his first novel, *December 12th*, in the governor-general of Korea's Korean language magazine, *Chosun*. The magazine was created by the Japanese to promote imperial Japan's colonial policies to the Korean citizenry. The novel was serialized that year in nine installments from February to December. In October, Mitsukoshi department store opened a branch in downtown Keijo (the Japanese empire's name for Seoul). This extravagant, neo-Gothic building still stands in Seoul, now owned by a Korean company. Its opening heralded the beginning of modern consumer culture in Korea. Yi Sang's reaction to this culture can be found throughout his work, including in the essay "A Journey into the Mountain Village" and in his early poem "AU MAGASIN DE NOUVEAUTES," which was written in Japanese and tentatively describes the interior of a department store whose description bears a striking resemblance to the Mitsukoshi building in Tokyo. The poem begins with the following lines: "The square in   the square in the square in the square in the square. / The   square   circle   of   the square circular motion of the square circular motion. [...] The eastern autumn that welcomes the fragrance of COTY unmoored from spring in MARSEILLE."

1931 Yi Sang entered the 10th Chosun Arts Exhibition with his Western-style painting "Self-Portrait." Around the same time, Yi Sang published his first Japanese poem, titled "ABNORMAL REVERSIBLE REACTION," and twenty other poems in the magazine *Chosun and Architecture*. While managing a construction site, Yi Sang fainted and was later diagnosed with tuberculosis. His essay "After Sickbed," published after his death, details his ordeals during this time in third-person narrative. Japanese invasion of Manchuria began in September. The war would continue into 1932 and end with Japanese victory. The annexation of Manchuria lasted until the end of World War II. Yi Sang's poems such as "Poem No. 12" of "Crow's Eye View" and "Street Outside Street" can be read as elliptical responses to the military violence of his time.

1932 Yi Sang's uncle Kim Yŏn-p'il, who had raised him and supported his education, died of an aneurism. Yi Sang continued to publish his Japanese writings in *Chosun and Architecture*, including the "Architecture Infinite Hexagon" series and "Publication Law."

1933 Worsening tuberculosis made it impossible for Yi Sang to continue to work for the governor-general. He resigned from his position and went to recuperate at a country hot springs resort. While there, he met a kisaeng (Korean courtesan) named Kŭm Hong. They returned to Seoul together, and Yi Sang opened a café in the downtown area in June. The café was named Jebi, a Korean word for the bird "swallow." Kŭm Hong and Yi Sang lived together briefly. A literary group known as Kuinhoe was formed around August in Seoul, and Yi Sang befriended core members of that group who frequented his café. At this time, with the help of Kuinhoe members, Yi Sang published his first Korean poems, like "Flowering Tree" and "This Kind of Poetry," in the magazine *Catholic Youth*. He was later welcomed into the group as a core member. Kuinhoe, which translates to "The Circle of Nine," was a nine-member group of poets and writers who wrote in vastly different styles about a variety of concerns. The group has since been recognized as the primary gathering of literary Korean modernists.

1934 Yi Sang began to serialize the "Crow's Eye View" poems in the newspaper *Chosun Central Daily*, where one of the Kuinhoe members worked as the editor of the arts section. It was his most daring publication yet, especially due to the highly experimental nature of the pieces. Due to protest and harsh criticism from the readers—which included "Stop this madman's ravings!"—the serialization was stopped at the fifteenth poem, even though thirty poems were planned to be published. Yi Sang later addressed his detractors in an unpublished editorial:

> Why do you all say I am crazy? We are decades behind others, and you think it's okay to be complacent? Who knows, I might not have enough talent to make this happen, but we really should be repenting for the time we've wasted dicking around. I am of different stuff than those gangs who think they are poets after writing a few here and there. I sweated picking these 30 poems out of 2,000 pieces that I wrote between 1931 and '32. I am sorry that after I began this series with a dragon's head, I won't even be allowed to attach a snake's tail, let alone a rat's tail, after so much rebuke and criticism. It was my mistake that I briefly forgot the stuffy rigidity of newspapers, but I still bow in gratitude to my friends Yi Tae-jun and Pak T'aewŏn for their support. I feel this is a foreshadowing of my new path, but I will not bow to anyone. I pity this wasteland where I can hear no echo for my howl! I won't ever try something like this again—sure, there is always some other method, but for now I will let this be. I will study quietly for a while, and in my spare time try to cure my insanity.

1935 Yi Sang's café was forced to close due to financial difficulties, and Kŭm Hong and Yi Sang ended their relationship. Yi Sang opened a few other cafés and bars around Seoul afterwards, but none of them proved successful. After failing at all his business attempts, Yi Sang went on a trip to Sŏngch'ŏn and Incheon. During this time, he wrote two essays, "A Journey into the Mountain Village" and "Ennui," which were both based on his trip. The first piece was serialized in a newspaper;

the second was published posthumously by his friends. After returning from his trip, with the help of his friends, Yi Sang started a job at a printshop that was run by his friend's father. After heightened censorship by the Japanese government, and numerous arrests of its core members, KAPF was disbanded.

1936 Yi Sang published Kuinhoe's first and only issue of the literary magazine *Poetry and Fiction* while working at the printshop. He also published the short stories "Spider&SpiderMeetPigs" and "Wings" and finally gained critical acclaim and attention from the literary community at large. He continued to publish his poems in newspapers and magazines; 1936 was his most prolific year. In June, he married Pyŏn Tong-rim. He began his married life in Seoul, but around the end of October, in search of a new literary world, he traveled to Tokyo. Earlier that year, Yi Sang's younger sister eloped with her lover and left Korea and moved to China. Yi Sang later published his letter to his sister, simply titled "A Letter to My Sister." In Tokyo, he met Korean poets and writers who were publishing the literary magazine *Three Four Literature*, which had a strong avant-garde bent. "I WED A TOY BRIDE" was published in it. It would be his last publication in life.

1937 In February, Yi Sang was arrested by the Japanese police in Tokyo for ideological crimes and was questioned and jailed for a month. His tuberculosis worsened to a point of no return, and he was moved to Tokyo Imperial University's hospital. On April 16, Yi Sang's father and his grandmother passed away. On April 17, he died in the hospital at age twenty-seven. His last words are purported to be either "I want to smell lemon" or "I would like a slice of melon." His wife was with him after traveling from Korea upon hearing that he was in critical condition, and she cremated his remains and brought them back to Korea. His ashes were interred in Miari cemetery, and their whereabouts have been lost.

烏瞰圖 李 箱 1

詩第一號

十三人의兒孩가道路로疾走하오。
(길은막달은골목이適當하오。)

第一의兒孩가무섭다고그리오。
第二의兒孩도무섭다고그리오。
第三의兒孩도무섭다고그리오。
第四의兒孩도무섭다고그리오。
第五의兒孩도무섭다고그리오。
第六의兒孩도무섭다고그리오。
第七의兒孩도무섭다고그리오。
第八의兒孩도무섭다고그리오。
第九의兒孩도무섭다고그리오。
第十의兒孩도무섭다고그리오。

第十一의兒孩가무섭다고그리오。
第十二의兒孩도무섭다고그리오。
第十三의兒孩도무섭다고그리오。
十三人의兒孩는무서운兒孩와무서워하는兒孩와그러케
뿐이모혓소。(다른事情은업는것이차라리나앗소)

그中에一人의兒孩가무서운兒孩라도좃소。
그中에二人의兒孩가무서운兒孩라도좃소。
그中에二人의兒孩가무서워하는兒孩라도좃소。
그中에一人의兒孩가무서워하는兒孩라도좃소。

(길은뚤닌골목이라도適當하오。)
十三人의兒孩가道路로疾走하지아니하야도좃소。

Poem No. 1

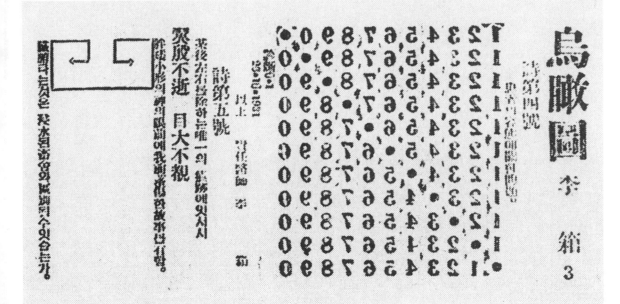

Poems No. 4 & 5

Poems

translated from the Korean by

JACK JUNG

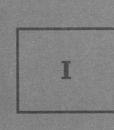

I

POEM no. 1

13 children speed toward the way.

(For the road a blocked alley is appropriate.)

The 1st child says it is scary.

The 2nd child says it is scary.

The 3rd child says it is scary.

The 4th child says it is scary.

The 5th child says it is scary.

The 6th child says it is scary.

The 7th child says it is scary.

The 8th child says it is scary.

The 9th child says it is scary.

The 10th child says it is scary.

The 11th child says it is scary.

The 12th child says it is scary.

The 13th child says it is scary.

Among 13 children there are scary children and scared children and they are all they are. (It is better that there is no other excuse)

Of those it is fine to say that 1 child is scary.

Of those it is fine to say that 2 children are scary.

Of those it is fine to say that 2 children are scared.

Of those it is fine to say that 1 child is scared.

(For the road an opened one is appropriate.)

It does not matter if 13 children do not speed toward the way.

———————

24 July 1934

POEM no. 2

When my father dozes off beside me I become my father and I become my father's
father and even then my father is my father like my father so why do I keep becom-
ing my father's father's father's······father why must I jump over my father and
why at last must I live and play the roles of myself and my father and my father's
father's and my father's father's father's all at the same time here—

25 July 1934

POEM no. 3

The one who fights is thus the one who hasn't fought and the one who fights has also been the one who doesn't fight therefore if the one who fights wants to see a fight then the one who hasn't fought seeing a fight or the one who doesn't fight seeing a fight or the one who hasn't fought seeing no fight or the one who doesn't fight seeing no fight matters not—

————
25 July 1934

POEM no. 4

Problem concerning the patient's face.

```
•  1 2 3 4 5 6 7 8 9 0
0  •  1 2 3 4 5 6 7 8 9
0 9  •  1 2 3 4 5 6 7 8
0 9 8  •  1 2 3 4 5 6 7
0 9 8 7  •  1 2 3 4 5 6
0 9 8 7 6  •  1 2 3 4 5
0 9 8 7 6 5  •  1 2 3 4
0 9 8 7 6 5 4  •  1 2 3
0 9 8 7 6 5 4 3  •  1 2
0 9 8 7 6 5 4 3 2  •  1
0 9 8 7 6 5 4 3 2 1  •
```

Diagnosis 0:1

26.10.1931

Diagnosis by primary doctor Yi Sang.

28 July 1934

POEM no. 5

A single trace shows erasure of both left and right.

GREAT WINGS FLIGHTLESS GREAT EYES SIGHTLESS

This is an old tale of a man collapsing before a short, fat god.

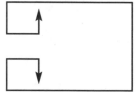

Can burning organs be distinguished from a drowning cattle shed?

28 July 1934

POEM NO. 6

Birdie parrot ✳ 2 horsies
                    2 horsies
            ✳ Birdie parrot is a mammal.

How I—I know of 2 horsies is how ah I do not know of 2 horsies. Of course I keep hoping.

Birdie parrot   2 horsies
"Is this little girl gentleman Yi Sang's bride?" "That is so"
Then I saw the birdie parrot turn livid. In my embarrassment my face reddened.

Birdie parrot   2 horsies
                    2 horsies

Of course I was banished. I didn't need to be banished. I dropped out on my own.
My body lost its axis and became so frail I quietly flowed my tears.
"There is there" "I" "My—Ah!—You and I"
"I"
SCANDAL is what? "You" "So it's you"
"It's you" "You" "No it's you" I got all
soaked and fled like a beast. Of course there was no—no one who knows or who saw but will that be so? Will even that be so?

———
31 July 1934

POEM NO. 7

There was a tree branch in the distant land of my banishment • A flower blossomed on this branch • It was a curious-looking flower blooming during the fourth full moon of the year • The world revolved and rotated thirty times • Two clean mirrors faced one another and circled each other as the world revolved and rotated thirty times • A full moon fell into the horizon, which was laughing together with budding leaves • Within a creek's powerful current the broken moon became utterly flustered after being sentenced to have its nose chopped off • A letter from home flowed into the distant land of my banishment • I barely caught it • Moon sprouted its faint light • The atmosphere covered up the idea of peace, made it distant from me in both time and space • I lived in the void for a year and four months in crushing poverty • A constellation limped and fell upside down in a dead-end alley, forcing a great blizzard to flee • Mud rain poured down • A rock of salt was dyed bloodred, shattered • My brain was the lightning rod for the bleaching of my bones • I was buried in the field like a poisonous snake imprisoned in his tower • I will never move again till the mercy of daybreak arrives

1 August 1934

POEM NO. 8 "ANATOMY"

1st experiment	Operation table		1
	Silver mirror		1
	Pressure	2 times the normal pressure	
	Temperature	Nonexistent	

First, we begin our work on the front of the anesthetized patient-subject, and project the subject's entire three-dimensional figure, which has solidity, onto the mirror. We apply liquid silver to the mirror from our side of reality, until the liquid silver permeates over to the other side. (Taking caution against radiation's penetration.) We slowly pull the subject out of anesthesia. We provide the subject with pen and paper. (The head researcher must avoid embracing the subject at all costs.) We release the subject from the operating room according to procedure. A day passes. We pierce the axis of the mirror and cut the mirror off from our side of reality. We apply liquid silver a second time.

 ETC We have not yet gained a satisfactory result.

2nd experiment	Horizontal mirror	1
	Assistants	Many

We choose the open field's truth. We attach the anesthetized extremities of the subject's upper body to the mirror's surface. We clean the liquid silver off from the mirror's surface. We pull back the mirror. (We hypothesize at this point that the projected image of the upper body of the subject wishes to go through the mirror at all costs) taking even the extremities of the subject's upper body with him. We apply liquid silver again (on the same side). At this point, we force out the void from the revolutions and rotations of the mirror. Until we requisition the 2 upper bodies completely. A day passes. We continue with the experiment. We continuously apply liquid silver to the same side of the mirror (the upper limbs are disposed) (or discarded) and so on. The silver mirror transforms, revolving and rotating again and again.

ETC All else unknown.

2 August 1934

POEM NO. 9 "MUZZLE"

The firestorm blows every day and a big hand reaches my waist at last. When the smell of my sweat soaks into the ecstatic valley of my fingerprints, shoot! I will shoot! I feel in my digestive machinery the heaviness of the barrel, and in my mouth the slick muzzle of a gun. I close my mouth to shoot but instead of a bullet blast— huh? What did I really spit?

3 August 1934

POEM NO. 10 "BUTTERFLY"

I see a dying butterfly on the torn wallpaper. A secret hole for connecting with the hereafter. I see the dying butterfly again, this time on the mirror's mustache. Its wings are drooping, and it eats the dewdrops of my breath. If I die while I close this secret hole with my hands, the butterfly will rise again as if from a brief rest, then fly away. Words like these must never slip out no matter what.

3 August 1934

POEM no. 11

The white porcelain cup looks very similar to my skull. When I hold the cup tightly, a strange arm suddenly sprouts from my arm like a tree, and the hand dangling on this new arm quickly picks up the porcelain cup and throws it down over my shoulder. But my arm is guarding the porcelain cup, which means that the shattered thing is in fact my skull. If my arm moves just as the tree arm slithers back into it, the white paper that was holding back the flood will be torn asunder. But my arm is still guarding the porcelain cup.

———————
4 August 1934

POEM NO. 12

The stained cloth flies away and falls midair. A flock of white doves. It is an announcement for the war's end and the coming of peace on the other side of this palm-sized sky. A massive flock of doves washes dirt from their feathers. On this side of the sky, a foul war begins, and the white doves are beaten to death with clubs. When ash darkens air, the white doves will fly away once again to the other side of the palm-sized sky.

4 August 1934

POEM NO. 13

My arm is cut off while holding a razor. When I examine it, it is pale blue, terrified of something. I lose my remaining arm the same way, so I set up my two arms like candelabras to decorate my room. My arms, even though they are dead, seem terrified of me. I love such flimsy manners more than any flowerpot.

7 August 1934

POEM NO. 14

On a grassy field in front of an old castle, I put down my hat. At the top of the castle, I tie a heavy stone to my memory and hurl it as far as I can. History weeps as it retraces the parabola. I look down at the castle bottom. A beggar is standing still like a totem pole next to my hat. The beggar is in fact above me. I wonder if he might be the specter of multiple histories in their combined form. The depth of my hat cries out to the desperate sky. Abruptly, the beggar bends his shaking body and throws a stone into my hat. I have already fainted. I see a map showing my heart migrating into my skull. A cold hand touches my forehead. My forehead is branded with the cold hand's mark. It will not fade until some time.

7 August 1934

POEM NO. 15

1

I am in a room with no mirror. Of course, the me-inside-the-mirror has gone out right now. I shudder in fear of him. Where did he go? What is he plotting to do with me?

2

I sleep on a cold bed, damp from embracing my crime. I am absent in my explicit dream and the military boot carrying a prosthetic leg dirtied my dream's white page.

3

I sneak into a room with a mirror. To free myself from the mirror. But the me-inside-the-mirror always enters at the same time and puts on a gloomy face. He lets me know he is sorry. Just as I am locked up because of him he is locked up shuddering because of me.

4

I am absent in my dream. In my mirror my counterfeit does not make an entrance. He craves my loneliness despite my uselessness. I have finally made up my mind to recommend suicide to him. I point him toward the viewless window. It is a window for suicide. But he instructs me that if I do not kill myself then he cannot kill himself either. The me-inside-the-mirror is almost a phoenix.

5

After covering my breast above my heart with a bulletproof shield I aim and shoot at my left breast in the mirror. The bullet goes straight through his left breast but his heart is on the right side.

6

A red ink is spilled from an imitation heart. In my dream I am late. I am sentenced to death. I am not the ruler of my dream. It is a great crime to seal up two humans who cannot even shake hands.

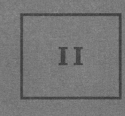

II

FLOWERING TREE

On an open field   a flowering tree stands   with no other like it   nearby   the flowering tree blossoms with a burning heart   as if thinking of   another flowering tree   burns its heart.   The flowering tree cannot reach the tree flowering in its thoughts   I wildly fled   for the sake of   one flowering tree   I truly did such weird mimicry.

July 1933

THIS KIND OF POETRY

While digging ground   for construction   I found a big stone   and looking at it
made me think it was shaped   like something from before   I must have seen
then workers carried it away   trashed it somewhere   I chased after   it was on
the sidewalk of a very dangerous road.

That night   because of heavy rain   the stone must have been washed clean   when
I went there   the next day   o how strange   no trace of it was left.   What stone
carried my stone away   in this pathetic thought   I composed.

"Beloved, I could live a lifetime and still never be able to forget you. I know you won't
grant me my turn with your love, but I alone will think of it now and for always. So
now and for always, I beg you be beautiful."

Because it was as though some stone   was ceaselessly looking up   into my face
this kind of poetry   I just wanted to rip apart.

———

July 1933

1933, 6, 1

That person lived   for thirty years   on a scale   (a certain scientist)   that other
person ultimately counted   over thirty thousand   stars   (as expected)   this
person here lived   for seventy years   no actually for twenty-four years   with no
shame   (I)

I   write an entry   on this day   in my autobiography   my autographed obituary
my body's flesh is now   never at home. Because it is proving too difficult   for me
to witness my body's poetry   get confiscated.

—————

July 1933

MIRROR

Inside the mirror is soundless
Perhaps no other world is so silent

◊

Inside the mirror I still have ears
Two pitiful ears cannot understand my words

◊

Inside the mirror I am a lefty who knows not
how to take my handshake—a lefty who knows no handshakes

◊

Because of the mirror I cannot touch the me-inside-the-mirror
Because of the mirror I get to meet the me-inside-the-mirror

◊

I do not have the mirror now but the me-inside-the-mirror is in it
I do not know but he is probably obsessed with his lefty work

◊

The me-inside-the-mirror is the opposite of me and yet

looks quite like me—I am disappointed

I cannot agonize over and examine the me-inside-the-mirror

October 1933

COMMON ANNIVERSARY

Before the battle sets the market street on fire

I am of course ignorant about Newtonian physics

I walk the street and see the mountain of apples in the store

I become as small as the bloodstain on my brain stem flunking physics every day

The girl never trusts me because I never trust girls and my words in falling motion

never affect the girl

The girl only stares at my words but not a word from my mouth falls on her eyes

Eventually the battle sets the market street on fire and I forget about the girl for

a long time because I have long discarded myself

I am filth and I let my dirty nails grow long

Not much happens at the refuge during this futile January

I obsess on sewing my worn-out clothes turned inside out

On a green paper pine tree branch stands a lonely white paper crane

When the fire pit is as bright as the sun it is as soft as the tropical spring and in

that corner I know all about memorializing the sphere's one full turn

July 1934

* WORDS * FOR * WHITE * FLOWER *

1

My face becomes a strip of skin before your face in moonlight
my words of praise for you are left unsaid but like a sigh they
tickle open a sliding paper door and creep into your hair smelling
like camellia fields and transplant seedlings of my sorrow

2

Wandering in a muddy field your high heels made holes
it rained and the holes filled with water and your lies and jokes
deepened my sorrow which I had prepared as a cup
of wine and a song for heaven which was ruined by your steps

3

When the moonlight sits on the straw mat on my back my blood
shaped like peppers trickles out from my shadow and my body's water
startled by moonlight turns into dewdrops in my arteries my raggedy
heart swallows bricks and you peer into it and call it a fish bowl

September 1934

The original Korean title is *So Yŏng Wi Je*. This translates to "Title (or Words) for *So Yŏng*." This particular name is not mentioned in any of Yi Sang's other writings. Literary Chinese characters for the name are 素 (So) and 榮 (Yŏng). The former character can mean "the first," "origin," "foundational," "white," and the latter can mean "glory," "honor," "flower."

DECORUM

Decorum
I

Like an anchor sinking into an ocean, a small sword of my torso is destroyed. When the small sword is totally gone, I find a dead small sword, abandoned at the same location.

Decorum
II

When the stern stranger and I sit next to each other, and stare at what is behind us, our spirits are confiscated from us. The final iron evidence of our ancestors' experiences forbids the stern stranger and me from having a relationship. In this calm darkness I let out the final joke from my mind, and any excretion is a secret. But, the stern stranger, whom I can never know, figures out my efforts and says he doesn't know anything. I am forced to worry even though we have been arranged at the end of the earth. It is difficult to clear my mind and stop worrying.

Decorum
III

The preserved skull has time to laugh but it has no muscle.

Decorum

IV

Who are you? You are outside banging on my door shouting "Open the door!" Even if I say you are not the heart looking for me—even if I say I don't know you—I still cannot let you stay outside. I try to open my door, and it is not just locked from the inside, but also from the outside. You don't know that so what's the use of opening it only from the inside? Who are you? Why were you born in front of a closed door?

Decorum

V

A tall and happy tree gives birth to a short child. This anemophilous tree's seed is dropped along the railway track, but it is always ostracized. When it grows into a shrub, it is weak, covered only with its baby leaves. The leaves eventually fall, and a snake gets caught under them. The snake gets thinner and thinner and sweats, while the mercury inside a glass thermometer shakes faintly nearby. I hear the sound of stakes being driven into the secret underground waterway.

Decorum

VI

Because the clock cuckooed, I looked at it and a wooden cuckoo came out. The cuckoo sat on the edge, but it couldn't have cried. It does not seem like it can cry at all. Did the precious cuckoo fly away?

April 1935

PAPER TOMBSTONE

I am tall, so my legs are long. My left leg hurts. My wife is short, so her legs are short. Her right leg hurts. With my right leg and her left leg, which are both healthy legs, we walk like one person. But, ah! Our legs limp without support. All's well with the world that is a hospital. A nameless disease always waits for its cure.

15 September 1935

PAPER TOMBSTONE

○ Paper Tombstone 1

My wife goes out to work every morning. Each day, she deceives men, even though the order she gets them might change. She says she does not receive more than one man a day. She says today is the day she will not return. I despair, but my wife casually returns with an expressionless, made-up face. When I ask my wife about her day, she tells me everything honestly. I quickly write into my wife's diary, which is definitely not part of my duty as her husband, what she could have lied about

○ Paper Tombstone 2

My wife must be a kind of bird. She gets so skinny, almost weightless, but she cannot fly because of the ring on her finger. In the evenings my wife always powders herself, and I feel like I am being mocked through the wall between our rooms. She never pecks on the grains of rice with her pale blue beak, even though she is wasting away. Sometimes, she opens the window and takes a look at the vast emptiness, but never twitters with her fine voice. My wife seems to have known how to fly and how to die at the very least, because she never leaves a footprint on earth. Her secret feet always have socks on; they are never shown to anyone else, but one day my wife actually disappears. Finally, I can smell bird droppings. The wallpaper is filled with scars from flapping wings. While cleaning up the scattered feathers,

I find the strangest thing in the world. It is a bullet! Ah! My wife is a bird! She swallowed it and sunk like an anchor. The bullet is rusty. It smells like hair and weighs thousands of pounds

○ Paper Tombstone 3

There is no nameplate for this room. The dog barks the other way. My wife has taken off her socks to mock me, and they look as hungry as I am. They are about to start walking. I seal the room and finally go out. At last, the dog looks back, and mourns one last time

BRAZIER

The freeze touches and desires to enter the room. The room endures. Holding on to the brazier, I struggle together with the book I am reading and pull on the house's main pillar. The freeze pushes in and the room's window caves in like a tumor. The brazier's fire goes out. Frozen inside what is barely a room, I lose my mind. Tides must be ebbing and flowing on a distant ocean. Suddenly, my mother sprouts from the room's finely tilled floor, takes the brazier from my wound, and carries it away into the kitchen. Outside, there was a tumult, I think, but a tree grows out of me. I stretch out my arms and block the window. Laundry clubs drum on my back—I am covered in rags. My mother carries off the freeze on her shoulders—it is a miracle. She brings back the brazier in her arms, warm like a cough medicine. She stands on my feverish body. My terrified book flees.

February 1936

37

MORNING

The midnight air ruins my lungs. Soot settles in. I make a fuss about my pain all night. Night comes and goes endlessly. Day breaks, when I can no longer remember what has been happening. Like a lamp inside my lungs, morning is turned on. I look around to see if anything has disappeared overnight. My habit has returned. I have ripped out many pages from my shamefully extravagant book. The early light carefully writes itself on my book's exhausted conclusion. As if the noseless night will never return.

February 1936

FAMILY

Though I keep pulling, the gate does not open, because my family inside is barely alive. Night fiercely scolds me. You have no idea how annoyed I am before the gate, where hangs a plaque with my name on it. I burn like a straw effigy in the night. My family is trapped inside the sealed door, but I cannot trade myself in. Frost comes down on our roof; the sharp needlelike tips on the roof are colored with moonlight. They tell me my family is suffering. One of them might be taking out a loan against the house. My family members are being pawned off one by one. I hang on to the gate's knobs like a drooping iron chain. Because I am trying to open the unopenable gate because I am trying.

February 1936

FORTUNETELLING

The fortuneteller pencil-sketches the basic outline of my life on paper. How can it be so sparse? I surrender my money and my past to this outline and enter its meaningless chatter. However, there are only promised handshakes with strangers. Luckily, I get to cover myself with some of the paper's blank space, but it is not the right size for me. I still manage to find an empty spot and stay there quietly as long as I want, but then my stomach aches. I have swallowed up all the painful pronunciations. I beat up the wicked paper and seize it by its collar, but the fortuneteller and the money vanish. My tired past sits alone with a blank look on its face. The fortuneteller returns and digs up dirt where my past is sitting, saying there should not be a seat there. My bad fortune now leans away from me—I want to be avenged, but it is a lost cause. The fortuneteller sees me living out my life from where he is sitting, then quietly runs away.

February 1936

PATH

I cough, spitting air into air with less strength each time. My story is this suffocating walk. My coughs are the punctuating marks made by my shoes. Tedious air decays those marks. I walk for about a page, but before I can cross the railway, I sense someone has been tailing me. A dagger cuts me down. Wounded, I meld with the railway, forming a cross. I collapse, dropping my coughs. After loud laughter, a pungent ink is spilled over my taunting face. My dropped coughs sit on my thoughts. They clamor. Stifling.

February 1936

III

STREET OUTSIDE STREET

Clamor grinds my body to nothing. Everyone says I am a boy, but I have an old face. Like an abacus bead punished for leaping out of its line, I barely hang on to my bridge and look down on a tranquil world below. Children as old as me giggle, gang up, and attempt to cross my bridge. Already, moonlight's weight is wobbling my bridge. Strangers' shadows are huge at first, then grow fainter, until they all collapse. Cherries ripen. Seedlings fade into smoke. My investigation leads nowhere —where is the applause I deserve? Perhaps this is a treason against my father. Silence—when I try to speak through my blocked pharynx, my speech sounds like a dialect. No—silence is clamor's dialect. I try to spill it all—my tongue's sharp edge probes my fresh bridge's center. Every day I rot, and my rotting follows a path, and an alley miraculously opens inside this path. My rotting flows in and comes upon a door of opulence. Inside the door are golden teeth. Surrounded by the golden tooth, a degenerate tongue dangles from diseased lungs. ∪—∪—. I can enter this alley, but I cannot escape its depth. Its depth begins to resemble my internal organs. A switched pair of shoes stagger over. Germs make my lower abdomen ache. Watery.

I ruminate. Because I am a crone. A sleep-inducing benefit of a disbanded government comes into view on a mirror in front of me. It is a dream—dream—dream that tramples on vain labor—this century's fatigue and bloodthirst spread out like the grid of a *baduk* board. My voracious lips secretly pretend to dine above such maliciously crumpled mire. Sons—many sons—their heavy shoes kick over the crone's wedding—the soles are made of iron.

When I climb down many stairs, wells become harder to find. I am a little late. Stale wind blows—school pupils' maps change colors daily. Far from home, the roofs of the houses have no choice but to shake. The colony is in its season of acne. People stagger and pour hot water on those who are sleep-talking. Thirst—the thirst is unbearable.

This ground was once the bottom of a primal lake. Salty. The pillars holding back the curtains become damp. Clouds do not come near me. My tonsils swell in the humorless air. There is a currency scandal—my hand, looking like a foot, shamelessly holds the crone's throbbing hand.

A rumor goes around about a tyrant's infiltration. Babies constantly turn into little grave mounds. The grown-ups' shoes hit other grown-ups' shoes. I never want to see them again, but where can I escape to? In a state of emergency, quarantined neighbors mingle. The distant cannon blasts and the blisters on our skins soothe us.

All I have here now is the stifling trash that came out of sweeping my vast room. Crows as big as suffocated doves once flew into my thunderbolt-infested room. The stronger crows tried to get out, but they caught the plague, and fell one by one. The room was purified, ready to explode. However, everything I have put down here is just my recent trash.

I go. A train car carrying Sun Tzu avoids my room. A note written in shorthand is laid out on my desk. There is also a cheap dish, and on the dish is a boiled egg—my fork bursts the egg's yolk. A bird, a medal, flies out—a wind from the bird's flapping wings tears up the grid. A flock of prophetic documents dances wildly on a field of ice. My blood wets a cigarette. The red-light district burns through the night. Fake angels begin to breed, flying every direction, covering up the entire sky. However, everything I have put here in my room is heating up, clamoring all at once. The vast room rots from within. The wallpaper gets itchy. The trash wildly sticks to my walls.

March 1936

CLEAR MIRROR

Here is a mirror—one page of it.
During a season, now forgotten,
my hair inside the mirror flowed down like a waterfall.

My tears do not make the mirror wet,
and the mirror does not bend even if I laugh at its face.
I see my ear
tightly folded like a rose.
I look in, and keep looking in—
the mirror's quiet world is pure.
No tepid fragrance reaches my nose.

Even after so many caresses, our hearts remain parallel
and it feels like a rejection.
Of course, my reflection's heart is on the right,
but it still must have a pulse,

so why am I turned down? I reach with my fingers—
a fingerprint blocks a fingerprint
and cuts me off.

During the month of May I desired

many times to be

on the road. Had I gone, I may have never returned.

If the mirror is like a page of a book

I will meet the season I once faced.

But the page remains here,

and the mirror—is its bookmark—

May 1936

○ **BAN**

I volunteer my strong dog for medical experiments. Injected with vitamin E, the dog tests poorly. The doctors beat my dog, because they are jealous of its biological superiority. Once, I longed to bark my heart out. Not anymore. In the medical school's empty courtyard, I stand tall and suffer being banned from the school. An abused skull appears on a thesis, but this world will never name it.

4 October 1936

○ PURSUIT

I shut all the windows and doors, so nothing that makes my wife happy enters. Every day and night, my dreams attack and petrify me. In darkness I catch the tail end of a certain smell, and pursue its traces throughout my house, which leads me to places I have never been. When my wife comes back from her excursions, she washes her face before entering our bedroom. She takes off many faces she resembles. I finally find her potent soap and hide it behind my back. Later, I tell her about my recent dream.

4 October 1936

○ DROWNING

Suicidal, my mind looks for a razor. The razor's blade is folded inside its grip and won't come out. Impatient, I roar at my razor and edge toward a cliff, desperate for a blade. I force the folded razor into myself, and suppress my pain, when suddenly its blade opens and grazes me. I bleed internally. However, I have nothing to cut my flesh open; there is no way for my evil spirit to escape. My body gets heavier because of my imprisoned suicide.

4 October 1936

○ CLIFF

I cannot see the flower. The flower is fragrant. The fragrance is in full bloom. I dig a grave in it. But I cannot see the grave either. I enter the grave I cannot see and sit there. I lie down. I can smell the flower again. I still cannot see the flower. The fragrance is in full bloom. I forget about it and dig a grave. I still cannot see the grave. I forget about the flower and go into the grave I cannot see. Ah, ah! I can smell the flower again. This flower I cannot see—this flower I cannot see.

6 October 1936

○ WHITE PAINTING

When I show the badge of virtue on my overcoat's lapel, I am allowed in. As the woman lets me in, she tells me she is also virtuous herself. She asks, So how about it? She wants to know how much I am worth in this world. I wag a crimson rag at this so-called chaste virtue of hers, and she gets mad. She begins to sweat like a turkey.

6 October 1936

○ LINEAGE

Even the buried white skull of my ancestor demands a full refund for his blood.
Moon brightens everything under heaven. Shuddering in fear, there is nowhere
under this sky I can hide. I want to tell the skull respectfully—Has it never occurred
to you that your legal seal has long become void?—I still carry in my body the sym-
biosis of our hateful transaction, like a legal seal. I cannot drain it out of me.

6 October 1936

○ LOCATION

At a location of significance, a sullen character induces a tragedy, but is there no stranger nearby? A tree—of alien language planted in a pot—wants to turn around and leave this place, while a chair acts deaf and refuses to move. I shove myself in between the tree and the chair like punctuation. So how can I make myself look responsible? As this tragedy gets annotated, I prepare my tears—no, I can't stand it anymore! I put on a hat and go out. But there is a stranger staying behind me, sitting on the chair, and he forgets to send my other self out.

8 October 1936

○ BUYING SPRING

My organ of memories begins to rot like a fish under the blazing sun. The following siphon effect happens to me—I can't make up my mind if I want three bananas at dawn and four at night, or vice versa. My mind is spent.

This exhaustion will be my fall, but I should not try to fight it. I should overcome it. An out-of-body experience. Shoeless feet shed their legs in the vacant heaven.

8 October 1936

○ LIFETIME

My bride's gloves sink down and turn into pebbles over my aching head. My aching head does not have enough strength to move out of the way of those cold, heavy stones. Still, I manage and make myself look regal like a queen bee. Caught beneath the stones, I will hate her as long as I live, though I cannot forget about my hands' dark abuses against her, and the red ants busily eroding away her life. Therefore, my bride faints every day, or perishes again and again like the bees. My aching head will never be able to move out of the way of her falling stones.

8 October 1936

○ INNARDS

My mouth is salty. My blood-soaked calligraphy brush must have rushed into my veins. Once, I took off my crumpled skin in repentance, but now it returns to me as blank paper, and a clot of blood has formed on its surface where the brush passed over. The torrential path of the brush is the indistinguishable combination of all my synereses. Salutations fill my closed mouth, and they are dark. An impotent thought tries to force my mouth open and fails. No testimony can be made at my trial. My past drowned and came apart in love, its shape destroyed, and became a crime. I faint in my body forever.

9 October 1936

○ BLOOD RELATION

The shabby man looks like Christ. His hardened heart makes me responsible for his death and his fate. Every hour, every minute, every second—he finds fault in me with his outdated ideas and threatens me. In the form of devoted filial love—I function precisely according to custom but remain constantly terrified. I am worried that if I do not assassinate this lumbering pretender Christ, then my lineage and my conspiracy will be plundered. I am running away to start fresh, but I cannot get rid of the stickiness in my inner ear.

9 October 1936

○ SELF-PORTRAIT

This is some country's death mask, rumored to be stolen. Its grassy facial hair fails to reach twirling adulthood in the far north, a mustache despairing and refusing to germinate. The ancient azure sky fell into the troughs of the death mask; now the final testament silently sinks into those traps like a stone monument. And then, foreign hands and feet parade past the death mask. The death mask is ashamed, having done nothing. The dignified meaning is crumpled.

9 October 1936

I WED A TOY BRIDE

Night 1

Sometimes, my toy bride's skin smells milky. She may be expecting a baby. I blow
out the candle and into her ear I chide,

"You are just like an infant."

My toy bride gets angry though it is dark. She answers,

"I went for a walk to the dairy farm."

Did my toy bride memorize the landscape during the day?

She is warm like the notepad by my breast. I keep getting skinnier, sniffing nothing
but milk powder.

Night 2

When I give my toy bride a needle, she pokes everything with it. My daily calendar.
My book of poems. My watch. My body, which is supposedly the residence of my
memories.

A thorn is growing inside my toy bride's mind—just like on a rose.

A blood spills from my light armor. To repair my wound, I eat a tangerine in dark-
ness. With nothing but a ring on her body, my toy bride looks for me. She draws the
darkness up like a curtain. She finds me right away. I mistake her ring for a needle
—it hurts.

My toy bride lights the candle and looks for my tangerine.

I ignore the pain and pretend not to care.

October 1936

IV

GIRL

The girl is clearly a photograph. She always remains still.

When her stomach aches, someone is playing tricks on her with a pencil. The pencil is poisonous. As if she swallowed a bullet, the girl turns pale.

When she vomits blood, a wounded butterfly is perching on her. She is a tree branch stretching out like a spider's web, tremulous under the butterfly's weight. The branch eventually breaks.

She stands in the middle of a small boat—away from the mob and butterflies. The frozen water pressure—the frosted glass panel's pressure takes away everything except the image of the girl. And many pointless readings begin. Inside a closed book, or in some crevice of a library bookshelf, the girl hides, as emaciated as paper. The girl's smell lingers in my metal printing types. A smudge from the girl's soldering iron stays on my book's cover. No sharp fragrance will lead me astray from recognizing—

People wag their fingers at me—the girl must be your wife! I don't want to hear it. It is a lie. Really, no man has ever seen the girl.

But she must become a wife to someone, anyone! Because the girl has given birth to something inside my womb—I have not yet excreted it. If I do not pull this disquieting knowledge out of myself—it will—like a coal blackening my body from within—it will corrode me.

I cremate the girl. Letting it all go. Whenever papers burn near my nostrils, the smell stays on forever and refuses to dissipate.

February 1939

PARAGRAPHS ON BLOOD RELATIONS

This raggedy man is almost a Christ. However, totally ignorant, he cannot speak as clearly.

It is the fifty-first ancestor worship day.

I must assassinate this imitation Christ. If I do not, all the signs foretell I will have my life confiscated.

The limping woman always approaches me, though she refuses to look at me. She demands I pay her back for my muscles, my bones, and my nearly depleted blood for their original prices. However, I don't think I have enough money. I write fiction that barely makes any. On the contrary, I want to demand compensation in medals for what I got from her. However—

How can she be so cruel? I have to run away from this hideous woman.

Only one ivory stick. Only one balloon.

From his grave, my ancestor's white skull gives me an ultimatum. He does not dare to even dream that his seal lost its power long ago.

(For his ultimatum, I will give up my brain functions.)

All the cells in a human body are replaced after seven years. Therefore, I will eat alone and never contact my blood relations. In seven years, I might be able to create a new bloodline. The bloodline will not exist for anyone, not even for myself—or should I stop thinking like this?

Or must I give back all of myself? No, I only need to vomit mud for seven years, like a goldfish. No—like a catfish.

February 1939

PARADISE LOST

Angels are nowhere to be seen. Paradise is an empty lot.

Occasionally, I meet 2 to 3 angels. One by one, they all give me a kiss. But then, they suddenly die on the spot. Just like bees.

There is a rumor of a war fought between angels.

I intend to tell Mr. B that I am going to dispose of an angel's corpse in my possession. People will laugh. In fact, someone like Mr. S will laugh hysterically. This is because Mr. S has faithfully preserved a precious, five-foot-tall angel's corpse for a decade—

Is there a cheerful flag to signal the angels to return?

I do not know why angels love hell so much. Perhaps the angels have figured out hell's appeal.

You can taste the poison in every shade of an angel's kiss. Once you are kissed, you fall ill then perish.

———————

February 1939

LOOKING GLASS

An iron-nib pen dangling on a spindle, an ink bottle, and a letter (there is enough of each for one person).

Nothing else. I am beginning to realize that it might be an unreadable text. His remaining body odor is trapped on the other side of the uncaring looking glass—making it impossible to investigate this tragic last scholar. He is in the still life of pen and ink and letter, as lonesome as Tutankhamen's tomb. No signs of happiness.

If we can have this scholar's blood, if his final blood cell still remains, then his life might be preserved.

Do we have his blood? Have you seen his bloodstains? There is no signature at the end of his esoteric opus. If he is who he is supposed to be, then he will come back.

Or he may actually be dead—he may have died being the final soldier—his honor undisputed—with all the glory. Tedious! Will he definitely return? Will he play tricks with his bony, fugitive fingers and move the still life of pen and ink and letter?

Even if he does, he will never be joyful. He will not babble. He will remain cold toward his ink as he turns it into literature. But, for now, he must be endlessly precise. The still life refuses pleasure.

The still life must be tired. The glass is pale. The still life reveals even his bones.

The clock's needles move leftward. What do their meters calculate? But the scholar, who is supposed to be himself, is probably weary. The calorie intake is reduced—organs have expiration dates. Almost, almost—it is a savage still life! Why won't this unbending poet return to us? Was he really killed in battle?

There is a still life in the middle of a still life. The still life cuts away at a still life in the middle of a still life. Is this not cruel?

The fingerprints on the mirror's glass lay siege to the clock's needles. They must be revived—to air out the tragic scholar's warnings.

———————

February 1939

MOON WOUND

The mustached man takes out a watch. I also take out my watch. He says, I am late. I say, I am late.

The Moon rises one day and a night late, dressed like a bleeding heart. Totally broken—the Moon may be hemophiliac.
The Earth reeks, choking my nose with sorrow. I walk in the opposite direction of the Moon. I worry—how can the Moon be so miserable—

I think of what happened yesterday—the darkness—and what will happen tomorrow—the darkness—

The Moon lags behind, refusing to march. My barely visible shadow wobbles up and down. The Moon can hardly bear its own weight, foreshadowing the menacing gloom of tomorrow. Now I must find some other word.
I must fight against the words of the Heavens, which are like the coldest winter. I must stay frozen between the iceberg and the snowy mountain. I must forget everything about the Moon—to discover a new moon.

Soon I shall hear a deafening noise. The Moon will fall. The Earth will bleed profusely.

People will tremble. They will swim in the Moon's evil blood and freeze.

Is this strange ghostliness infiltrating my bone marrow? Perhaps only I will be able to sense the final tragedy on the Earth, which even the Sun has abandoned.

I finally chase down my galloping shadow and get in front of it. Now, my shadow chases me as if it is my tail.

The Moon is in front of me. New—new—like a flame—or perhaps like a rapturous flood—.

———

February 1939

ABOVE: Cover for *Chosun and Architecture*, designed by Yi Sang.
Yi Sang's poems written in Japanese were published in this journal.
FACING: "Memorandum on the Line" 1–3.

三次角設計圖

金海卿

◇線に關する覺書　1

	0	9	8	7	6	5	4	3	2	1
1	●	●	●	●	●	●	●	●	●	●
2	●	●	●	●	●	●	●	●	●	●
3	●	●	●	●	●	●	●	●	●	●
4	●	●	●	●	●	●	●	●	●	●
5	●	●	●	●	●	●	●	●	●	●
6	●	●	●	●	●	●	●	●	●	●
7	●	●	●	●	●	●	●	●	●	●
8	●	●	●	●	●	●	●	●	●	●
9	●	●	●	●	●	●	●	●	●	●
0	●	●	●	●	●	●	●	●	●	●

（宇宙は冪に依る冪に依る）

（人は數字を捨てよ）

（靜かにオレを電子の陽子にせよ）

十倍百倍何十倍何百倍何億倍何兆倍すれば人は數十年數百年數千年數萬年數億年數兆年の太古の事實が見れるじやないか、それを又絶えず崩壊するものこするか、原子は原子であり原子であり原子である、牛理作用は變移するものであるか、原子は原子でなく原子である、放射は崩壊であるか、人は永劫である永劫を生き得ることは生命は生でもなく命でもなく光であることであるのである。

臭覺の味覺と味覺の臭覺

（立體への絶望に依る誕生）

（運動への絶望に依る誕生）

（地球は空棄である時封建時代は涙ぐむ程懐かしい）

一九三一、五、三一、九、一一

◇線に關する覺書　2

1＋3
3＋1
3＋1　1＋3
1＋3　3＋1
3＋1　1＋3
　　　3＋1
　　　　　1＋3

線上の一點　　A　B　C
線上の一點　　C　B　A
線上の一點

二線の交點　　A＋B＋C＝A
三線の交點　　A＋B＋C＝B
數線の交點　　A＋B＋C≡C

一九三一、九、一一

◇線に關する覺書　3

∴ $_nP_r = n(n-1)(n-2)\cdots(n-r+1)$

3	2	1		1	2	3
●	●	●		●	●	●
		●		●		
		●		●		

（腦髓は扇子の樣に圓迄開いた、そして完全に廻轉した）

一九三一、九、一一

たこにあることを思ふこ樂しい、幾何學は凸レンズの樣な火遊びではなからうか、ユウクリトは死んだ今日ユウクリトの焦點は到る處において人文の腦髓を枯草の樣に燒却する收斂作用を羅列することに依り最大の收斂作用を促す危險を促す、人は絶望せよ、人は誕生せよ、人は絶望せよ、人は誕生せよ、人は絶望せよ、人は誕生せよ

（太陽光線は、凸レンズのために收斂光線こなり一點において爀々こ光り爀々こ燃えた、太初の僥倖は何よりも大氣の屑と屑とのなす屑をして凸レンズたらしめなかつ）

スペクトル

軸X　軸Y　軸Z

速度etcの統制例へば光は秒毎に三〇〇〇〇〇キロメートル逃げることが確かなら人の發明は秒毎六〇〇〇〇〇キロメートル逃げられないことはキツトない。それを何

ABOVE: "Memorandum on the Line" 4, 5, and beginning of 6.

FACING: "Memorandum on the Line" end of 6 and all of 7.

原子構造としてのあらゆる運算
の研究。

方位と構造式と質量としての数
字の性状性質に依る解答と解答の
分類。

数字を代數的であることにする
ことから数字を數字的であること
にすることから数字を數字である
ことにすることから数字を數字で
あることにすることへ（1234
567890の疾患の究明と詩的
である情緒の乗場）

数字のあらゆる性状　数字のあ
らゆる性質　このこれらに依る数
字の語尾の　活用に依る　数字の滑
減。

算式は光と光よりも迅く逃げる
人さに依り運算せられること。

人は星——天體——星のために犠牲
を惜むことは無意味である、星と
星との引力圏と引力圏との相殺に
依る加速度函數の變化の調査を先
づ作ること。一九三一、九、一二
よ。

◇綠に關する覺書 7

空氣構造の速度——音波に依る——
速度らしく三百三十メートルを模
倣する（何んと光に比しての遅だ
しき劣り方だらう）

光を樂めよ・光を悲しめよ、光
を笑へよ、光を泣けよ。

光が人であると人は鏡である。

光を持てよ。

——

（観覺のナマエを持つことは計量
の嚆矢である。観覺のナマエを發
表せよ。）

□ オレノのナマエ。

イ　オレの妻のナマエ。（既に古い
過去においてオレの AMOURE
USE は斯くの如くオレに聰明であ
る）

ソラは観覺のナマエについての
み存在を明かにする（代表のオレ
は代表の一例を擧げること）

蒼空、秋天、蒼天、青天、長天
一天、蒼穹（非常に窮屈な地方色
ではなからうか）ソラは観覺のナマ
エを發表した。

観覺のナマエは人と共に永遠に
生きるべき数字的である或る一點
である、観覺のナマエは運動しな
いで運動のコヲスを持つばかりで
ある。

観覺のナマエは光を持つ光を持
たない、人は観覺のナマエのため
に光よりも迅く逃げる必要はな
い。

観覺のナマエを發表せよ。

観覺のナマエらを健忘せよ。

人は光よりも迅く逃げる速度を
調節し度々過去を未來において淘
汰せよ。一九三一、九、一二

人は光よりも迅く逃げる速度を

◇診　断　0：1

或る患者の容態に關する問題。
```
1 2 3 4 5 6 7 8 9 0 ・
1 2 3 4 5 6 7 8 9 ・ 0
1 2 3 4 5 6 7 8 ・ 9 0
1 2 3 4 5 6 7 ・ 8 9 0
1 2 3 4 5 6 ・ 7 8 9 0
1 2 3 4 5 ・ 6 7 8 9 0
1 2 3 4 ・ 5 6 7 8 9 0
1 2 3 ・ 4 5 6 7 8 9 0
1 2 ・ 3 4 5 6 7 8 9 0
1 ・ 2 3 4 5 6 7 8 9 0
・ 1 2 3 4 5 6 7 8 9 0
```
診斷 0：1
26・10・1931
以上　責任醫師　李　箱

"◇ Diagnosis 0:1."

Poems

translated from the Japanese by

SAWAKO NAKAYASU

INTRODUCTION TO THE
JAPANESE POEMS OF YI SANG

SAWAKO NAKAYASU

Yi Sang's former residence is located just west of the Gyeongbokgung Palace, a heavily touristed part of Seoul, Korea. My last visit here was in 2017. The palace grounds were teeming with tourists, many dressed in traditional hanbok they had rented for the day. Though I at first interpreted this as an act of blithe cultural appropriation, I quickly realized that a majority of the participants were Korean tourists. I was wrong about the cultural appropriation, though some variant scent of it remained in the air.

*

One of Walter Benjamin's metaphors for translation says, "While content and language form a certain unity in the original, like a fruit and its skin, the language of translation envelops its content like a royal robe with ample folds."[1] Indeed translation often reflects a translator's admiration, or perhaps their desire to "wear" someone else's text—to try it on, like the hanbok-wearing visitors at the royal palace. The "ample folds" signal an acceptable looseness: even when the royal robes are the correct size, they will never fit *exactly*, like fruit to its skin. In Yi Sang's case, his relationship to the Japanese language was mandated by colonization—thus certainly not based on admiration—and yet his poetic use of the colonial language manifests an internal and intralingual translation of sorts, taking place even before the moment of writing. Just as he wrote *in* Japanese from a locale *outside* of it, Yi Sang mirrors the position of the translator being on the *outside* of an "original" text (or language), while on the *inside* of the new "translation" (or language). Desire and opposition embed themselves into this third space between languages. In the book *Treacherous Translation*, in which Serk-Bae Suh discusses translation in colonized Korea, he notes: "Just as colonialism maintains differences between the colonized and colonizers while claiming to erase them, translation simultaneously points to the gulf between two languages while trying to bridge the gap."[2] Yi Sang's Japanese-language poetry is a blend of avant-garde techniques with his own idiolectical assertions. Together they both point to and bridge this gulf, as a colonial, internalized variant of translation.

*

Yi Sang is now an established figure in Korea's modernist canon, but he was not as well known during his brief life, which took place entirely under Japanese rule. He was forced to learn Japanese at school, and could initially only publish in Japanese. And yet, it was also via the Japanese language that Yi Sang gained exposure to the modernist poetry and art movements that significantly influenced his work. In Yi Sang's poems, the combination of colonial circumstance and engagement with modernist experimentation catalyzed a certain inflection on that experimental mode. Thus his work contributes to the formation of a more robust understanding of global modernisms.[3]

Modernist poets in Japan in the 1920s and 1930s pulled elements of Western art and culture and integrated them into their own rapidly shifting artistic landscapes. Although Yi Sang had no personal connections to these poets, it is interesting to note that his poems quite clearly aligned with their aesthetics. One line in Yi Sang's poem, "Memorandum on the Line 6" (1931) reads:

To make it so that numerals are numerals from the fact that it is so that numerals are numerals from the fact that it is so that numerals are numerical from the fact that it is so that numerals are algebraic . . .

This circular syntax calls to mind the cubism-inflected repetitions in Gertrude Stein's writing, as well as Kitasono Katue's iconic line, "ocean of the ocean of the ocean of the ocean . . ." ("Magic," 1929).[4] Likewise this line—"The square in   the square in the square in the square in the square"—is the opening to Yi Sang's playful "AU MAGASIN DE NOUVEAUTES" (1932). Referring to the French "novelty store," the precursor to the modern department store, Yi Sang's architectural mind seems to translate into language the individual, "square" shops nested within the larger, squarish architecture of the department store. The Mitsukoshi department store was home to Japan's first escalator in 1914, and when they opened a branch in Seoul in 1930, it featured elevators. The vertical movement of people is described in Yi Sang's poem:

The people who went down from above and up from below and down from above and up from below are the people who did not go up from below or down from above or up from below or down from above.

The poem is, as were many poems by his Japanese contemporaries, also populated with a colorful assortment of surreal imagery: "castrated socks," "A sugar cube with black INK spilled on it," as well as, in the penultimate line, "The GOODBYE that rises up near the RADIATOR."

Yi Sang's poems are conversant with those of the Japanese modernists, but through them he also repurposes the tools of the avant-garde as instruments of rebellion. As Japanese poets sought to break from their own traditions, it is possible that Yi Sang was also seeking ways to push against the loss, erasure, and invisibility of colonial circumstances. While it is often said that translation stretches the target language by virtue of accommodating a new text, here Yi Sang was stretching Japanese to make it accommodate his position as a colonial subject. In that sense, avant-garde aesthetics may have provided the perfect cover for his subversive distortion of Japanese language conventions.[5]

*

In the orthographic conventions of the time, most Japanese literature was written in a combination of Chinese characters and the hiragana script, whereas the katakana script was mostly used for foreign-language words and for official documents.[6] Yi Sang's poetic lexicon includes recently imported vocabulary from European languages, as was common practice among his Japanese avant-garde contemporaries. In his early poems, Yi Sang inverts standard Japanese orthography, writing the foreign words (like "slipper," "table," and "tungsten") in hiragana rather than katana. Thus he normalizes that which would otherwise be delineated as foreign, and puts the rest of the otherwise "native" script in that of the foreign. Never mind the fact that the mere incorporation of such vocabulary was already a defamiliarizing, radical move by the Japanese poets—Yi Sang pushes the concept to its edges. In my English translation, I chose small caps to represent the katakana script, and all caps to represent words originally written in roman script. By mimicking the blocky uniformity of the characters, I signal its difference from the familiar, rounded hiragana script. The use of capital letters also evokes the language of the telegram, itself a stiff style that finds resonance in Yi Sang's idiolect.[7]

When it came to the use of Chinese characters, Yi Sang chose to use traditional (and thus complex) Chinese characters, which were still in use in Korea, but not in Japan. The effect on the Japanese reader is that they are legible, but different.

One of the few Japanese poets who similarly used traditional Chinese characters was Anzai Fuyue, cofounder of the journal *A* and one of the founding editors of the influential monthly journal *Shi to Shiron* (Poetry and Poetics). Anzai, too, had a relationship to colonialism: as a child he had moved with his family to Dalian, China, which was then a territory under lease by Japan. Beyond the orthography of his own poems, the fact that Anzai was a founding editor of *Shi to Shiron* also speaks to the notion that the avant-garde movement in Japan was not only influenced by Western movements, but was also shaped by myriad forces, including contact with Asian languages as a by-product of colonialism.[8]

*

The Japanese avant-garde poet Hagiwara Kyojiro, a contemporary of Yi Sang, was known for his heavy use of graphic design elements in his poems. Yi Sang's poems on the other hand incorporated graphic elements into the syntax of the poetic line itself. Thus a number of poems from the "Abnormal Reversible Reaction" series feature a triangle as the subject or object of a sentence, resulting in lines like "△ IS MY *AMOUREUSE*" ("FRAGMENT SCENERY," 1931). It not only disrupts the expectations of syntax (also making the poems challenging to read aloud), but altogether rejects the lyric "I," the gendered and hierarchical Japanese "I," deploying instead the abstract or symbolic language of math in naming a subject (here potentially read as "delta," signifying "change" in mathematical terms) that resists fixed identity.

His style is also marked by the use of nonpoetic, mathematical language and symbols, sometimes grafted onto words, as with the prefix "CO" in "CO-CLERICAL," or "CO-SKY." His twists of idiomatic syntax create mismatches in positive and negative parts of speech, producing awkward phrases such as "NOT KIND OF A TERRIFYING THING," or the transformation of nouns ("FOSSIL") into transitive verbs

("FOSSILED," as opposed to "FOSSILIZED"). There are playful puns, such as the word "sentimentalismED" (in "ABNORMAL REVERSIBLE REACTION") as a pun on "centimeter" in this poem laced with architecture jargon. Many of his choices limn the border of experiment and error, and many of my decisions as a translator are an attempt to maintain this ambiguity.

In "Poem No. 1" of "Crow's Eye View," which is perhaps Yi Sang's most famous poem, thirteen children are found running, and scared.[9] These scared, running children, through a slight slip of syntax, are both scary children and scared children. The poem torques a single word in such a way that it slips into syntax error, one that renders the children "scary." The extent to which the children are scary feels parallel to the extent to which the cognitive dissonance of the colonial condition underlies the logic of Yi Sang's Japanese-language poems. It is operational, but a little askew.

*

From the palace where I first encountered the hanbok-wearing tourists, I made my way to Yi Sang's former residence, which has been converted to a hybrid café and memorial site, designed in homage to the café that Yi Sang himself had operated. There is a room in the back dedicated to the memory and exhibition of his life and work. On that spring day in Seoul, as I quietly sipped a cup of coffee, a group of children rushed in. They noisily filled up the tiny space, and then in a matter of minutes were gone. Decidedly not scary, nor scared, they were quick to set off for their next destination.

1. Walter Benjamin, "Die Aufgabe des Übersetzers," trans. Harry Zohn, in *The Translation Studies Reader*, ed. Lawrence Venuti (Routledge, 2000), p. 19.

2. Serk-Bae Suh, *Treacherous Translation: Culture, Nationalism, and Colonialism in Korea and Japan from the 1910s to the 1960s* (UC Press, 2013), p. xvi.

3. His work is discussed in the "Korean Modernism" chapter of *Global Modernists on Modernism: An Anthology*, ed. Alys Moody and Stephen J. Ross (Bloomsbury, 2019).

4. Kitasono later returns to a similar structure in his postwar poetry, where his poem "Monotonous Space" (1959) ends with the lines, "white square / in the / white square / in the / white square / in the / white square / in the / white square" (my translation).

5. The critic Kawamura Minato also notes that certain lines in Yi Sang's poems directly expressed anticolonial rage (such as "IT DOES NOT GROW AND IT DOES NOT DEVELOP AND / THIS IS AN OUTRAGE," or "I PERSIST IN INDEPENDENCE BUT" albeit cloaked in modernist pyrotechnics). Incidentally, he also uses the metaphor of "fancy clothing" to describe the donning of modernist language by Yi Sang. See "Toukyou de shinda otoko" *Gendaishitecho*, vol. 29, Issue 11 (1986), p. 148.

6. For example, the Japanese constitution at the time was written with Chinese characters and katakana, whereas in the postwar revision, it replaced katakana with hiragana.

7. My decisions in English-language orthography also reflect the differences between poems. In "LE URINE," for example, the Japanese version uses fairly standard orthography, with French words (in all caps) sprinkled therein, so the translation does likewise.

8. Toshiko Ellis, "The Topography of Dalian and the Cartography of Fantastic Asia in Anzai Fuyue's Poetry," *Comparative Literature Studies*, Vol. 41, No. 4, East-West Issue (2004), pp. 482–500.

9. In his fascinating reading of Yi Sang, "Jean Cocteau in the Looking Glass: A Homotextual Reading of Yi Sang's Mirror Poems," Walter K. Lew considers the "terrified" or "terrifying" children as likely to be a translation of Jean Cocteau's *Les Enfants Terrible*, published in Japanese translation in 1930. *Muae: a Journal of Trans-cultural Production*, Vol. 1: 118–149.

ABNORMAL REVERSIBLE REACTION

CIRCLE OF ANY RADIUS (MARKET PRICE OF PAST PARTICIPLE)

LINE CONNECTING POINT ON INTERIOR OF CIRCLE TO POINT ON EXTERIOR
OF CIRCLE

TEMPORAL INFLUENCE OF TWO KINDS OF EXISTENCE
(WE ARE INDIFFERENT TO THIS)

HAS THE LINE MURDERED THE CIRCLE

MICROSCOPE
UNDER WHICH THE ARTIFICIAL, JUST LIKE THE NATURAL, WAS PHENOME-
NALIZED

      ×

AFTERNOON OF THE SAME DAY
OF COURSE THE SUN WAS NOT MERELY IN OCCUPATION OF THE PLACE IT
WAS REQUIRED TO BE BUT IT WAS ALSO NOT IN BEAUTIFICATION OF THE
PACING THAT NEEDED TO BE SO.

IT DOES NOT GROW AND IT DOES NOT DEVELOP AND
THIS IS AN OUTRAGE.

A BUILDING OF WHITE MARBLE ON THE EXTERIOR OF THE IRON FENCING
MAJESTICALLY STOOD
AND FROM A SERIES OF bars WITH A CENTER DISTANCE OF 5 CM
THE DISPOSAL METHOD RESERVED FOR FLESH WAS sentimentalismED.

A PURPOSELESS LENGTH   REMAINED COMPOSED

WHEN THE SUN SHONE DOWN UPON THAT SWEATY BACK
A SHADOW WAS CAST ON THE FRONTSIDE OF ITS BACK

THE PEOPLE SAID:

"That constipated patient yearns to crawl into the home of that wealthy man to receive some salt."

....

———
1931, 6, 5

FRAGMENT SCENERY

△ IS MY *AMOUREUSE*

I GAVE UP AND CRIED

THE LAMPPOST PUFFED A CIGARETTE

▽ IS I/W

        ×

O ▽! I SUFFER

I PLAY

▽'S slippers ARE NOT THE SAME AS CANDY

IN JUST WHAT WAY AM I EXPECTED TO CRY

        ×

THINKING ABOUT THOSE LONELY FIELDS

THINKING ABOUT THAT LONELY DAY OF SNOW

I AM NOT THINKING ABOUT MY SKIN

I AM A RIGID BODY AGAINST MEMORY

▽ IS MY DREAM

AS OPPOSED TO THE FACT THAT YOU SHOULD HAVE HIT MY KNEE SAYING

"Perhaps you might sing together"

REALLY

A cane! YOU ARE LONELY AND FAMOUS

WHAT DO I DO

         ×

AT LAST I BURIED ▽ IT WAS A SNOWY LANDSCAPE

———————

1931, 6, 5

▽'S GAMES——

△ IS MY *AMOUREUSE*

IF IT IS SO THAT A PAPER SNAKE IS A PAPER SNAKE

▽ IS A SNAKE

▽ DANCED

LAUGHING THE LAUGHTER OF ▽ WAS UNPRECEDENTED AND WAS FUNNY

Slippers NOT LIFTING OFF THE GROUND IS NOT KIND OF A TERRIFYING THING

▽'S EYES ARE HIBERNATION

▽ LEARNS THAT THE LIGHT IS A THIRD-RATE SUN

     ×

WHERE DID ▽ GO

IS THIS THE top OF THE CHIMNEY

MY BREATHING IS NORMAL

AND SO THEN WHAT IS tungsten

(NOTHING)

A CURVED LINE

THAT MAKES PLATINUM EQUIVALENT TO THE COEFFICIENT OF REFLECTION

HAS ▽ GONE TO HIDE UNDER THE table

        ×

1

2

3

3 WAS HEADED TO CONQUER THE COMMON MULTIPLE

THE TELEGRAM HAS NOT ARRIVED

―――――――

1931, 6, 5

BEARD

(BEARD • BEARD • ALL THOSE THINGS • THAT QUALIFY AS FACIAL hair)

1

THERE IS AND WAS A LAUGHTER THAT WAS A FOREST IN THE PLACE WHERE EYES
ARE SUPPOSED TO BE

2

CARROT

3

American GHOSTS ARE AQUARIUMS BUT ARE QUITE ELEGANT
THEY ARE ALSO SOMBER AT TIMES

4

BY THE MOUNTAIN STREAM—
A DEHYDRATED PLANT-BASED
AUTUMN

5

THE FACT THAT THE SOLDIERS OF THE FIRST PLATOON ADVANCED TO THE EAST
AND WEST
NEEDS TO BE A MEANINGLESS THING
BECAUSE THE ATHLETIC FIELD KEEPS EXPLODING AND FISSURING

6

THREE-CENTERED CURVE

7

Flour SACK FULL OF MILLET

IT WAS AN EASY FLEETING MOONLIT NIGHT

8

AT ALL HOURS I KEPT PLOTTING TO STEAL

AND IF THAT HAD NOT BEEN THE CASE AT THE VERY LEAST I WAS A BEGGAR

9

THAT WHICH IS SPARSE IS OPPOSITE TO THAT WHICH IS DENSE AND

THAT WHICH IS ORDINARY WAS OPPOSITE TO THAT WHICH IS EXTRAORDINARY

MY NERVES HAD HOPED FOR A MAIDEN MUCH MORE CHASTE THAN A PROSTITUTE

10

HORSE—

SWEAT—

$$\times$$

IT IS ACCEPTABLE TO LIKEN A WALK TO CO-CLERICAL WORK

THUS TIRING OF THE BLUE OF THE CO-SKY-LIKE EXCLUSIONISM

———

1931, 6, 5

HUNGER—

NO SNACK BAG IN MY RIGHT HAND   I SAID

AND BACKTRACKED 5 LI ON THE PATH I JUST CAME IN SEARCH OF THE SNACK BAG

CLUTCHED BY MY LEFT HAND

                    ✕

THIS HAND HAS FOSSILED

THIS HAND NO LONGER WANTS OWNERSHIP OF ANYTHING WILL NO LONGER EVEN

FEEL THE OWNERSHIP OF THAT WHICH IS OWNED

                    ✕

IF THE THING IN THE PROCESS OF FALLING RIGHT NOW IS SNOW   THEN MY TEARS

THAT JUST FELL SHOULD BE SNOW

MY INTERIOR AND EXTERIOR AND

EACH AND EVERY MIDPOINT REGARDING THIS SYSTEM IS FRIGHTENINGLY COLD

LEFT   RIGHT

THESE HANDS ON EITHER SIDE FORGET THEIR OBLIGATIONS TO EACH OTHER

AND NEVER AGAIN SHAKE HANDS

AND UPON THIS ROAD THAT NEEDS CLEANING THAT IS FULL OF DIFFICULT LABOR

SPRAWLED ABOUT I PERSIST IN INDEPENDENCE BUT

IT MUST HAVE COLD

IT MUST HAVE COLD

        ×

WHO POINTS AT ME AND CALLS ME LONELY

JUST LOOK AT THIS RIVALRY OF WARLORDS

JUST LOOK AT THIS WAR

        ×

I FALL INTO A STUPOR IN THE MIDDLE OF THE FEVER ATTACK OF THEIR DISCORD

TEDIOUS MONTHS AND YEARS FLOW BY AND I OPEN MY EYES TO SEE

I IMAGINE A QUIET MOONLIT NIGHT AFTER THE CORPSES HAVE EVAPORATED

O INNOCENT DOGS OF THE HAMLET   DON'T YOU BARK

MY BODY TEMPERATURE IS IRRESPONSIBLE AND

MY HOPES ARE SWEET INDEED.

1931, 6, 5

◈ TWO PEOPLE · · · · · 1 · · · · ·

Jesus Christ began his sermon in shabby clothes.

Al Capone captured the Mount of Olives for what it was and went on his way.

         ×

Sometime after the 1930s———.

At the neon-lit entrance to a certain church, a chubby Capone sold tickets while stretching and shrinking the scar on his cheek.

1931, 8, 11

◈ TWO PEOPLE · · · · · 2 · · · · ·

Al Capone's money is indeed very glossy and almost as shiny as a medal, but Jesus Christ's money is unbearably dilapidated and anyway does not even take one step beyond the bounds of what would qualify as money.

It is a well-known and unsurprising fact that Jesus Christ rejected to the end the frock coat that Capone had urgently sent him.

1931, 8, 11

◈ LE URINE

A wind blew in like a flame, however however there is indeed a lens like ice. Melancholy is pure white like the DICTIONAIRE. The green scenery casts a blank expression upon the retina and so anything all goes on in a grey and cheerful way.

To creep across the treacherous back of a fieldmouse-like earth was to emaciate who started it in the first while caressing the stunted ORGANE while the heart that reverses the empty pages of a history book is a peaceful bookworm. Meanwhile what was that, if it was not the case that it had to have been a stringy fairy tale carried along albeit in modest increments together with the most insipid and holiest of smiles from the place where archaeology as it gets entombed is at last not obliged to taste sexual desire.

Harmlessly the flat and deep-green species of serpent and harmlessly the swimming fluidity of glass extort from one nameless mountain that is not a peninsula fluidity like an archipelago and then the transparent air of the place that spits out the amazement and mystery and also anxiety together is there cold like in the northern lands, but just look at the sunlight. The crow takes flight just like a peacock and fakes before the light dies a common outline differing not in the least from diamonds upon half a celestial body with disorderly sparkling scales owning them without arrogance.

Is it such that in the very slight amount of brain matter that had lost the COMBINATION of numbers in the shuffle, when the flowers bloom atop the lip of the nap-

state at the exotic atmosphere that is blameless like sugar, the bustling flowers all depart whithersoever and the little wood-carved sheep mourns both legs of this and is listening quietly and intently to something.

Because of the steam with no moisture, every possible suitcase dried up and the holiday saltwater bath near the insatiable swimming beach in the afternoon is the circular music and rest notes sadly split apart like a banana-leaf fan, O dance, Sunday Venus, O sing, with shaggy voice, O Venus of Sunday.

On that peaceful dining-hall door was a white transparent sign that said MEN-STRUATION and the limitless phone was exhausted and placed upon the LIT, the white cigarette still hanging out of its mouth.

Maria, O Maria, Maria with the black skin, where have you gone, boiling water seeps gradually out of the bathroom faucet but go and quickly fend off last night, I do not want to eat so please put my slippers up atop the gramophone.

Countless rain hits hits countless eaves. Should I try eating the already-faded lunch that was likely made by the collaborative fatigue of the upper arm and the forearm—I do. The mandolin packs itself up and is held by the hand with the cane and if it is to exit those small wooden gates then when and what time do we get word that the incense-like twilight no longer did come, O rooster, preferably could you crow quietly head hanging low before the police get here, the fact of the sun sabotaging for no reason as much as it wants needs to remain completely outside of the case at hand.

1931, 6, 18

◈ MOVEMENT

I climb up above the first floor to the second floor to the third floor to the rooftop garden and look to the south and there is nothing there and look to the north and there is nothing there and so I go down from the rooftop garden to the third floor to the second floor to the first floor and the sun that rose in the east has set in the west rose from the east and set in the west and rose from the east and set in the west and rose from the east and it is in the middle of the sky and I take out my watch and look and see that it has stopped although it is the correct time but the watch is younger than I am or rather I am older than the watch is and it can't be helped that that is what they will think of me because that is probably the case and so I threw away the watch.

———

1931, 8, 11

◈ **MEMORANDUM ON THE LINE 1**

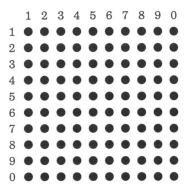

(The universe depends on the exponent depends on the exponent)

(People should discard their numbers)

(Quietly adopt me as the proton of an electron)

Spectral

X-axis   Y-axis   Z-axis

Regulation of speed etc. for example if it is certain that light escapes at 300,000 km per second then it is most likely impossible that the invention of people are unable to escape at 600,000 km per second. And if you multiply that by how many tens hundreds thousands millions billions trillions then we can see the truths of several tens hundreds thousands millions billions trillions of years of the ancient past, and then do we consider it something that constantly decays, an atom is an atom is an atom is an atom, do physiological effects mutate, an atom is not an atom is not an atom is not an atom, does radiation mean decay, that people live through an eternal eternity means that life is not living nor is it life but it is light and it is it is.

Sense of taste of sense of smell and sense of smell of sense of taste

    (Birth dependent on despair for the solid)
    (Birth dependent on despair for movement)
    (When the earth is an empty nest I am so nostalgic for feudal times my eyes well up)

_____

1931, 5, 31, 9, 11

◇ MEMORANDUM ON THE LINE 2

1+3

3+1

3+1 1+3

1+3 3+1

1+3 1+3

3+1 3+1

3+1

1+3

One point A on the line

One point B on the line

One point C on the line

A+B+C=A

A+B+C=B

A+B+C=C

Intersection of two lines   A

Intersection of three lines   B

Intersection of multiple lines C

3+1

1+3

1+3 3+1

3+1 1+3

3+1 3+1

1+3 1+3

1+3

3+1

(The convex lens converges the rays of the sun into a point that burns up brilliantly, the sheer chance of the beginning of the world was above all the layer made between one atmospheric layer and another layer and there is pleasure in thinking of the fact of not being the thing that makes it a convex lens, isn't geometry like playing with a convex-lens-like fire, today when Euclid is dead the point of convergence for Euclid was everywhere prompting the danger of prompting the greatest convergence action of the enumeration of the convergence action that burned the brains of humanity like dead grass and, O people despair, O people be born, O people be born, O people despair.)

1931, 9, 11

◇ MEMORANDUM ON THE LINE 3

```
  1 2 3
1 ● ● ●
2 ● ● ●
3 ● ● ●


  3 2 1
3 ● ● ●
2 ● ● ●
1 ● ● ●
```

$\therefore {}_nP_n = n(n-1)(n-2)\ldots\ldots\ldots(n-n+1)$

(The brain opened into a circle like a folding fan, then rotated completely)

_____

1931, 9, 11

◇ MEMORANDUM ON THE LINE 4 (DRAFT)

A bullet sped through the cylinder (correction of the logical fallacy that the bullet sped through in a straight line)

Hexagonal sugar (a.k.a. sugarcubes)

The spongy fillings of the waterfall (literary interpretation of the waterfall)

1931, 9, 12

◇ MEMORANDUM ON THE LINE 5

When people escape faster than the light do people see the light, people see the light, they marry twice under the vacuum of age, do they marry three times, O people, escape faster than the light.

Escape to the future and look at the past, escape to the past and look at the future, or escaping to the future is not the same as escaping to the past and escaping to the future is escaping to the past. O those who grieve the expansion of the universe, live in the past, escape into the future more quickly than light.

People once again welcome me, people at the very least meet the much younger me, people welcome me three times, people at the very least meet the young me, wait appropriately, people, and then enjoy *Faust*, it is not that Mephistopheles is mine but is me.

Morning adjustment of speed, people collect me, we do not speak, it is not long before the present that listens closely to the past becomes the past, the past that repeats, the past that listens closely to the past, the present prints only the past and the past aligning with the present is the same as regards those other multiple cases.

Make fresh suggestions, know the past as present, people come to know old things as new things, O forgetfulness, eternal memory loss will rescue all the memory loss.

I come and thus I unconsciously align with people I escape faster than people the new future is newly here, people escape quickly, people pass through beyond the light and in the future they wait to ambush the past, O people first welcome one of me, O people kill me upon a congruent figure.

O people, learn the techniques of the exercises of the congruent figure, otherwise what do you plan to do with the scattered pieces of myself of the past.

Eat the fragments of thought, otherwise the new thing is incomplete, kill the suggestions, people who know one thing should halt the next thing after knowing one thing knowing three things, should make everything so to know one thing after knowing one thing.

O people—escape once all at once, escape to the maximum, before people are born twice before they are xx'd, people withhold from escaping quickly out of fear of seeing from the future the beginning of the world of their ancestor's ancestor's ancestor's galaxy's galaxy's galaxy, people escape, they escape quickly and live eternally and caress the past and from the past again they live in that past, O childlike innocence, childlike innocence, insatiable and eternal and childlike innocence.

———
1931, 9, 12

◇ MEMORANDUM ON THE LINE 6

Azimuthal study of numerals

  4   ᔦ   ᔅ   Ᵽ

Mechanical study of numerals

Temporality (Historicity based on popular thought)

Speed and coordinates and speed

  ᔅ + ᔦ

  ᔦ + ᔅ

  4 + Ᵽ

  Ᵽ + 4

  etc

People are the eternal hypothesis of something, just like the non-phenomenalizing of static mechanics, people should discard the objectivity of people.

Concave lens based on the convergence of systemic subjectivity.

4 Fourth generation

4 Born on the twelfth day of the ninth month in the year one thousand nine hundred thirty-one.

4   Association and selection of proton and proton as proton nucleus

Research into every calculation as atomic structure.

Solutions and classification of solutions based on the natural characteristics of numerals as bearing and structural formula and mass.

To make it so that numerals are numerals from the fact that it is so that numerals are numerals from the fact that it is so that numerals are numerical from the fact that it is so that numerals are algebraic (The dumping grounds for poetic affect and for the investigation of the disease of 1 2 3 4 5 6 7 8 9 0)

(Every characteristic of numerals   Every property of numerals   The annihilation of numerals based on the application of word endings of numerals based on these things)

The mathematical formula is forced into a mathematical operation based on light and the people who escape faster than light.

It is meaningless for people to regret their sacrifice for the sake of the stars—celestial bodies—stars, they must first create an inquiry into the changes in acceleration functions based on the cancelling out of gravitational fields and gravitational fields of the stars and the stars.

──────────

1931, 9, 12

◇ MEMORANDUM ON THE LINE 7

Speed of air structure—based on sound waves—emulates three hundred thirty meters in the form of speed (what an exceedingly inferior performance compared to that of light)

Enjoy the light, mourn the light, laugh the light, cry the light.

When light is people, people are mirrors.

Wait for light.

———

To hold the NAME of vision is the opening whistle of planning. Announce the NAME of vision.

□ MY NAME.

△ MY wife's NAME (already in the distant past my *AMOUREUSE* is intelligent in such a way)

Prepare the passage for the NAME of vision, and then bestow utmost speed upon it.

———

The SKY makes clear the existence only of the NAME of vision (as the representative I am to represent with one example)

Blue sky, autumn sky, azure sky, blue sky, long sky, one sky, large sky (quite a narrow set of regional colors) the SKY announced the NAME of vision.

The NAME of vision is a single point is numerical it should live eternally among people, the NAME of vision does not move but it does hold the COURSE of movement.

———

The NAME of vision holds the light does not hold the light, there is no need for people to escape faster than the light for the sake of the NAME of vision.

Just forget the NAMES of vision.

Conserve the NAME of vision.

People should adjust the speed of escaping faster than the light and repeatedly weed out the past from the future.

———

1931, 9, 12

◇ AU MAGASIN DE NOUVEAUTES

The square in   the square in the square in the square in the square.

The   square   circle   of   the square circular motion of the square circular motion.

The person who sees through the smell of the soap of the blood vessels that the soap passes through.

The earth made in imitation of the globe made in imitation of the earth.

Castrated socks. (Her NAME was WORDS)

Anemia cells. YOUR EXPRESSION IS ALSO LIKE THE LEGS OF A SPARROW.

The enormous weight that drives itself towards the diagonal of the parallelogram.

The eastern autumn that welcomes the fragrance of COTY unmoored from spring in MARSEILLE.

Mr. Z's vehicle cruising the clear sky like a bird. It says Roundworm Medicine.

Rooftop garden. The young MADEMOISELLE imitating a monkey.

The formula for a falling body speeding straight through the curved straight line. Two wet bits of dusk pressed as XII on the dial.

The GREETING from the fitted door from inside the CANARY in the birdcage in the DOOR inside the DOOR.

The male or female friends who arrive at the entrance to the cafeteria split apart.

A sugar cube with black INK spilled on it is carted atop a tricycle.

Military boots stepping on a business card. Fake nasturtium that runs through the town.

The people who went down from above and up from below and down from above and up from below are the people who did not go up from below nor down from above nor up from below nor down from above.

The bottom half of that woman is like the top half of that man. (I am one who mourns the chance meeting of sadness)

A square case starts walking. (THAT IS A STRANGE THING)

The GOODBYE that rises up near the RADIATOR.

Rain outside. Group migration of luminescent fish.

◇ DIAGNOSIS 0:1

Problem concerning the condition of a certain patient.

```
1  2  3  4  5  6  7  8  9  0  •
1  2  3  4  5  6  7  8  9  •  0
1  2  3  4  5  6  7  8  •  9  0
1  2  3  4  5  6  7  •  8  9  0
1  2  3  4  5  6  •  7  8  9  0
1  2  3  4  5  •  6  7  8  9  0
1  2  3  4  •  5  6  7  8  9  0
1  2  3  •  4  5  6  7  8  9  0
1  2  •  3  4  5  6  7  8  9  0
1  •  2  3  4  5  6  7  8  9  0
•  1  2  3  4  5  6  7  8  9  0
```

Diagnosis 0 : 1

2 6 • 1 0 • 1 9 3 1

End of Document   Attending Physician: Yi Sang

Yi Sang (LEFT) with writer Pak T'ae-wŏn (CENTER) and poet Kim So-un (RIGHT).

Essays

translated from the Korean by

JACK JUNG

A JOURNEY INTO THE MOUNTAIN VILLAGE

1

I have been without the fragrant taste of MJB coffee[1] for almost twenty days. Newspapers are rarely delivered out here. Instead, the postman occasionally brings local stories printed on the packaging papers of hadorong hue, coarse and brown.[2] The stories are about the complicated lives of silkworm cocoons and corn. The folks here worry about one of their families living far from the village, and I worry about what I left behind in the city.

They say deer and wild boar live on P'albong Mountain across the village. Some swear they saw bears hunting crayfish in the creek, where folks held rain rituals in the past. I keep fantasizing that those animals on the mountain are zoo animals that have been set loose. At night, when it is moonless and utterly black, P'albong Mountain disappears like someone going into their blankets.

But, because the air here is crystal clear, I can read my beloved Gospel of Luke with starlight alone. Far away from the city, the stars double their numbers. It is so silent here that I might be able to listen to the celestial movements for the first time in my life.

I turn on the gasoline lamp inside my room at the inn. Its smell is like the evening paper in the city. I am carried back to the dreams of my boyhood with it. Dear Jung, my brother! Do you remember how we used to smoke cigarettes underneath the gasoline lamps? A grasshopper just jumped up and landed on the top of my lamp. Its green color writes the letter *T* on my drowsy dream and underlines my most peculiar memories. The grasshopper lowers its head—as if in grief—and I listen to its throatful song. It sounds like a bus conductor girl's clipper punching through each passenger's ticket. It also sounds like the snapping of barbershop scissors. I close my eyes and listen closely.

I bring out my notebook, and with an ink of wild-grape shade I write a few rough lines to capture the poetry of this mountain village.

A butterfly with its stained wings rips
yesterday's newspaper—
The balsam flower is shaped like my beautiful lover's ear,
inside her ear is a vision of news from our past.

Time passes, and my throat's parched. I drink the cold water I left beside my bed. The water has sunken into its cup like a deep sea. A scent of minerals drifts up from the cup and passes through my lungs like mercury moving inside a thermometer. If I am asked to draw the chilling arc of the liquid's passage through my body, I think I will be able to.

The sound of the starlight shining down on the blue-tiled roof of this inn is like earthenware jars breaking in the middle of winter. The bugs are clamorous, because autumn is coming. The autumn arrives so quickly that I can barely write it down on postcards. Do I have what it takes to comprehend the light and the shadow of this moment? The beating of my pulse transforms my room into a clock; the long and short needles turn inside me. They tickle my eyes one at a time. The smell of oil drifts in and out of my nose. Underneath the lamp, I begin to doze off.

First, I dream about a city girl who looks like the logo of Paramount Pictures. But then, I see my poor family I left behind in the city. They stand in line like the prisoners of war in photographs. I worry again. I awake from my dream.

Should I kill myself? I look at my raggedy jacket hanging on the nail of my room's wall. Oh, it has come all the way with me here! How many endless miles of western provinces did we travel together!

2

I straighten the lamp's wick then light it and with my fountain pen begin to sow drops of navy blue ink on a paper. Miserable human mouths are born on each ink drop. The paper gets crowded with such mouths—.

I tell myself, *Tomorrow I will try to enjoy looking at flowers all day. I will rub away my worries with an alcohol-soaked cottonball.* Because my dreams have been so troubling, I want to dream a dream filled with blossoming flowers, a dream of gravure of primary hues, like a colorful picture book. I would like to compose a refreshing poem, in a 7-point font, for each illustration of my dreams.

I have a splendid home in the city, but I cannot see it right now past P'albong Mountain's broadleaf trees. The steel utility poles reach all the way up to the waist of P'albong Mountain, but their wires transmit in codes only the headlines of newspapers.

In the morning, the inn's yard is pestered by the sun, and the noise wakes me up. The day has come to the yard like baggage not yet unpacked, and a bright-red dragonfly flies in circles like a disease in the sunlight. I forgot to turn off the lamp in my room. The trace of last night lingers as a button of my old vest. This button is the doorbell that will allow me to visit the night again. I take off the coldness of my body from the night and go out, then come upon a flower garden in the corner of the yard. There grow fiery cockscombs and balsam flowers.

Perhaps these flowers are sucking up the ground's fever from deep below, and then heating up the air I breathe with their blossoming. The balsam flowers are used to dye the fingertips of young girls. I see a few that are white petaled among this bevy of reddish balsam flowers. I wonder if white balsam flowers will also dye fingertips—but I remember how even the white petals dye everything in the fine shade of red madder.

Orange-colored citrons hang from the flower garden's straw fence. They mingle with the peanut vines. Together, the citrons and vines appear as sepia-toned scrolls on a folding screen. At the end of the fence, there is a pumpkin vine. Pumpkin flowers are plain yet bold. Spartan honeybees loiter on them. Reflecting lemon yellow colors, the bees are splendid, arrayed in gold like a scene from a Cecil B. DeMille film. When I listen closely to the bees' wings, I can hear the rickety fan inside the parlor of Renaissance Café in Seoul.

There is yet another plant here. It looks like an asparagus leaf, which I usually find in a vegetable salad. I ask the innkeeper's child about it. The child tells me it is a kisaeng[3] flower. I ask him, "What will it look like when it has fully blossomed?" The child answers that it will look like scarlet silk.

Upon hearing this, my mind recalls the beauty of the city's kisaeng. O how they wear their short Josette skirts—they were once banned by our ancestors! How the Westminster cigarettes seem bound to their lips! The girls smack their lips, scented with Wrigley's chewing gum, and the smell is sweeter than mint. Their chewing sounds like the pages of a thick ledger being flipped through. But, the kisaeng flowers here in this village look like the girls one might see in Hyewŏn's paintings.[4] Or, I think they also look like the kisaeng from the postcard illustrations we saw when we were boys—women on rickshaws holding up scarlet umbrellas.

Pumpkins have ripened. Hot rice cakes are made from the pumpkin slices and radish—their good steamy smell is what our great grandfathers' ghosts from the countryside visit us for on Lunar New Year's Day and Hanshik Day.[5] The pumpkins' dignified shapes and hues make me think about the foundations for our country's next century; they also seem to be waiting for the rugby-carrying forearms of this generation's young warriors.

When the citrons ripen, their skins come apart, and their insides ooze out. I pick one of them from the vine and hang it inside my room. I lie down beneath its voluptuousness as the juice drips down on me. I hope that my emaciated pencil-like body will be fattened by this juice. However, the funny-looking citrons, which are neither vegetable nor fruit, have no fragrance. The smell of the city still lingers on my flesh. I use the soap beside my washbowl to take this smell off from me, layer by layer. Now the same smell hovers in my room and won't leave me.

3

At the entrance of a small, overgrown passage that goes up P'albong Mountain, there is a commemorative monument for someone named Mr. Ch'oe, and another tombstone for the everlasting remembrance of a certain Mr. XXX. Their stones stand there like postage stamps. I hear that Mr. Ch'oe and that other person are both alive and well in the village. Isn't that ridiculous?[6]

Suddenly, I want to see a church. I want to repent before a god who loves even the farmers of this village, though they live tens of thousands of miles away from the Holy City of Jerusalem. My footsteps lead me toward where I hear hymns being sung. Underneath a poplar tree, a goat is tied down. Its beard is grown in an old-fashioned way, streaming down beneath its chin. I go up to it and look into its wise eyes. They are clear and wise and beautiful like exquisite marbles made of cellu-loid, wrapped in edible starch Obulato paper.[7] The painted edges of its eyes move. The goat looks down on my meager countenance, my pitiful physiognomy.

Nearby, a cornfield looks like a great military parade. When wind blows, I can hear multitudes of armors scraping against one another. The carmine tassels of military caps bend backward and sway. A gunshot rings out from P'albong Moun-tain. It must be the ceremonial gun salute, but it is actually the sound of an air rifle, a bullet piercing the liver of a small bird. Dogs of different colors emerge from the cornfield: white, yellow, black, grey, and another white. Row after row. The *sensual* excitement of the season adds to the splendor of this Cossack parade.

Wild ginseng dissipates, its remnants flowing down the creek. On the stepping-stones, the cabbage leaves can be found. They are usually washed before being made into kimchi. Freshly seasoned kimchi's crisp taste reminds me of *Smile* eye-drops. I squat on the shiny granite stepping-stones. My body forms a crooked N shape. Two young country maids carrying water jars hesitate. I feel sorry and stand up, but I walk in their direction as they come over the stepping-stones. I brush past them. I can smell greens from their skins that is as brown as hadorong paper. Their cocoa-colored lips are wet with wild grapes and gooseberry. Their eyes, in which the purified azure sky is preserved, do not look at me.

The socks that the *sweet girl* wore in the Misono cosmetics advertisement at the M department store had the same color as the skin of these country maids—the color of barley. I think about the new women of the city fancily donning their super-streamlined hats, and their *handbags* with thin straps like a leash on a cat's stom-ach. I think about the worm-like fingers of the pale factory girls in the city, who emerge on the asphalt roads at dawn. The delicate skins of city girls of different classes are not stained with wealth or poverty. Instead, the heavy smudges of all kinds of fingerprints press on their skins.

4

I want to know more about the plump country maids, who have skin that is as strong as flawless muslins, though they are poor. They do not suck on chewing gums or chocolates. Instead, they suck on the seeds of sweet ground-cherries. I want to bless them, but I cannot see the church. The church has shyly hidden itself in the grass from the devious eyes of this city man, and only the ringing of the bell lingers like a scent. Perhaps it was nothing, only my restless soul haunted by a phantasmal noise.

There is a tall mulberry tree in the middle of a millet field. Young maids are there to pick the mulberry, and they climb up the tree like cable technicians. The maids are pure whiteness, the most desirable fruits, fully ripened. Two maids are up in the tree, and one remaining below fills up their baskets with what her friends pick and toss down. I feel as though I am watching a stage play based on a folk song, in which a handful of plump mulberries is enough to fill up a whole basket.

The millet ears have all dried up and died. They are as light as cork. They lower their heads. Oh, let it rain! I want to suck up water like a sponge. The cloudless sky seems to have banned rain, yet it remains blue and soft. It is impossible for the shallow roots of the millets signaling SOS to reach the river flowing beneath the bedrock.

Two boys take off their rubber shoes and dip their feet in the creek's water and start fishing. The creek is a vein of the Earth, filled with spite. What kind of fish could be living in this ominous, powerful water? The creek pierces Earth's feverish body and flows toward sloping fields. A rumor of autumn blows in the wind.

It is indeed time for autumn to come. Can you not hear how it is whispering to us, "Is it okay to come now?" The millet ears rustle. It sounds the same as the gentle bow a bride gives to her guests at her wedding. The crafty old wind urges the millets to ripen. However, the young millets' hearts are blue and restless.

Who messed up the millet field—did you mess up the millet field—because you didn't think they were going to make it to autumn? This field is such a mess. Silkworms—in every house there are silkworms. The silkworms are thicker than the millet ears, eating up the mulberry leaves in a blink of an eye. Their voracious appetite is as lofty and luxurious as queens'. For the young maids, mulberry picking is the ultimate glory of their bodies, their lights flowering. However, they have now picked all the mulberries. As if all their dowries have been completely spent, the young maids' passions are suddenly directionless.

The dark night calls for them, and the young maids go out of their houses in their nightgowns. They go to where their pinkish cheeks lead them—their trophy is laid beside the mulberry tree. All they need to do is to reach there. They tread on the millet field. Their feet deliciously browned by the ultraviolet rays are the scrummage that breaks the millet ears. In autumn, in that season of high skies and plump horses, with reverent hearts soaring toward the heavens, the young maids fatten the silkworms as if the worms are noble and sacred livestock. Theirs is a juicy *romance*. All this makes me think of Collette's story *La Chatte*.

5

While on the village street, I hear a sewing machine, and sneak a peek into a house next to the school where the sound is coming from. A girl with long, braided hair caresses the sewing machine with her naked feet, and the machine starts to giggle, as if the thin thread brushing against its waist is tickling it. Through its laughter and teasing, the famed silk of this province is woven. Around fifteen silk cloths come together, turning into dresses to be worn for the memorial rites at the ancestral graves. They also wash away the sorrows of married life. They are dreams, and also the dustpans that collect the dreams. Such is my nonsensical, delightful fancies.

In a room inside the cigarette store, twilight has set in already. Amidst these gloomy gallons of air stands a fresh evergreen tree. This foreign tree looks like an immigrant who lives only in twilight. On the tree hang numerous fruits, slender and white. They are cocoons of silkworms. Neatly picking these fruits of latest wisdom, any of the young women could be our country's Mother Mary. They look like the evangelizing paintings of Pietàs, a mother weeping for her dead son, as they deconstruct this *Christmas tree* of silkworm cocoons.

Cosmos flowers are blossoming in the schoolyard, and the students are learning new words. Using a simple arithmetic, they convert their honesty and innocence into guile and deviousness. It is a mournful way to pay for the price of modernization. Like the pages torn out of a family's genealogy book, two white butterflies fly in circles meaninglessly right above the flower garden that is pungent with white-chalk smell. A stopper on a tennis-ball tube is opened, and its pop echoes across the schoolyard. That pop is like a point on the contour lines the teacher draws on the board during an economics class. Tonight, in this same schoolyard, there will be a film showing, paid for by the village's chamber of commerce. Film? The darling of this century. It is the victorious eighth art that reigns over all other art forms. How can its peerless and debauched attractiveness be comparable to anything else? However, the folks here in this village hold a childlike notion about films. For them, the moving pictures are the result of the ingenuity of a fellow countryman who may or may not have learned this magic from some red-haired barbarians.

I am always left with the plain taste of the void after watching a film—Zhuangzi's butterfly dream must have been like this. Oh, how many times has my flat, round head become a *camera*, filming with my tired *double lenses* the early autumn scenery of ripening corn, then projected it—my film is a thin sorrow flowing as *flashbacks* of fragmentary stills—I send them now to my lonely fan who yet remains in the city.

6

Night has arrived. It is near the tenth day of the month, and the moon rises early in the evening. The village people, who seem to have stepped out of legendary folktales, gather in the schoolyard and lay out their straw mats. They might as well be Antarctic *penguins* who tilt their heads beside a gramophone. The outdoor silver *screen* looks like a sheet of paper on which a short, but a long, life will be written down—it is the screen in the twilight, a substitute for a *biography*. There is a city woman lodging now at an inn across the one I am staying at. I can hear the symphony of provincial accents from the schoolyard.

The film starts. A pier bridge in Busan appears. Next shot is the Moran Peak in Pyongyang. The steel bridge over Yalu River passes like history. Applause and cheer—famous directors of the Occident will have to hide their faces in shame, because their works will never get the same reactions from these villagers. During the ten-minute intermission, the president of the village's chamber of commerce gives an additional speech, translated from Japanese into Korean.

The moon is behind the clouds. It feels as if smoking has been banned. The spotlight shines on the face of the speech-giving president. All the mountains, streams, plants, and grass may be reeling away from how frightening he looks. The countryfolk here have never seen an electric lamp, other than the headlights on automobiles. Caught in that blinding ray of light, the pale president steps down from the podium. None of the unenlightened villagers give applause to any part of the president's speech. Of course, I cannot help but be one of them.

Past eleven o'clock at night, the film appreciation comes to a happy ending. The financial association members and the projectionist hold a party at the only proper diner in this village. I return to my inn and straighten the wick of my dying lamp and begin to read. The book was written by Goda, and it was lent to me by an old gentleman staying next door to me in this inn. He gave it to me as a lesson, hoping that its words will cure my laziness and depression. It is a rare book titled *The Way of Humanity*. A dog is barking ceaselessly from a distance. The villagers cannot easily forget the intense *high-color* experience of the film, and are unable to depart from the schoolyard.

Clouds pass, and the moon is out. The bugs are loud. It is as if the window of a dance hall has been left open. I have a city person's nostalgia to worship all my fellow wayfarers. Women who are fresh like the covers of new magazines—gentlemen who are as old as their neckties—my pale-faced friends—my home that does not wait for me. For all of them, I want to rewrite the words of my naked body and send them to the city. I fall asleep—in my dream, the metal types at a printing press are jumbled while they are being set up to print the Bible. The printer's apprentice thoughtlessly puts them back together. I become the disciple who gets drawn and quartered. I renounce my starving family, not just three times but ten times.

My worrying is bigger than the world that erases me. When I open the floodgates, the tides of my worrying percolate through my ruined body. However, I have not yet pulled open my *masochistic* bottle cap. My worrying engulfs me, and, meanwhile, my body withers away as if the wind and the rain are whittling at it.

I spread the night's sad air on the top of my paper and write a letter to my pale-faced friend. In the letter, I have sealed my own obituary.

September-October 1935

1. Popular brand of American ground coffee.

2. Hadorong is a made-up word that Yi Sang seems to have come up with on his own. This is the only time we see it used in the literature of his time. It is a wordplay that imitates the sound of the English word "hard-rolled," which refers to industrial, brown, coarse papers that are now often used for grocery bags or other packing.

3. Traditional Korean courtesan women.

4. Hyewŏn Sin Yunbok was a nineteenth-century royal court Korean painter from the late Chosun Dynasty. While his official court artworks have not survived, his smaller paintings that often satirize the lives of gentlemen-scholars of Korea remain popular. Many of his works depict affairs between scholars and courtesan women. He also painted portraits of courtesan women that focus on their beauty.

5. Also known as Cold Food Day. It is when memorial rituals for the ancestors are held, around early April, and fresh grass is planted on ancestral graves.

6. Yi Sang here is mocking the practice of reserving one's gravesite. The belief in p'ung-sujiri, or the theory of divination based on topography, was and still is a strong influence in Korean culture. Where one would be buried influencing the fortunes of one's family is part of this practice, and thus places in the mountain that are regarded as good spots according to this theory were reserved by people for their eventual graves.

7. A brand of transparent starch papers used to wrap powder medicine for easy consumption.

ENNUI

1

It'd be better—if it got dark—quickly—but the summer days of this remote village are so murderously tedious and long.

P'albong Mountain stands to the east of me. Its lines have no curves; how can a mountain be so dull looking?

I look to the west and see nothing but the fields. I look to the south and it is the same. I look to the north, and it is still just fields. O—these endless fields—what are they up to? How can they be so utterly, singularly green?

There are about ten farmhouses on the main street of this village. The writhing pine trees are used as the pillars of these houses; their walls are a dried mixture of rubbed mud and straw; their fences are made of corn stalks; pumpkin vines cover up the fences. All the houses look the same to me.

The same cypress tree I saw yesterday; I will see Mr. Kim again today; I will see the same white dog, the same black dog again and again tomorrow.

The boiling sun strikes down on the rooftops, on the fields, on the mulberry trees, and on the hens' tails. This unbearable heat bombardment continues all day long.

I have just had breakfast. There is nothing else to do. But, out of nowhere, a blank paper known as "today" is spread out before me. The paper demands that I write some sort of a news article. I have no choice but to do something. I must research what I am going to have to do. Well then—shall I go to Mr. Ch'oe's porch and play chess with him? I think I might like that.

Mr. Ch'oe is out in the fields. At first, I don't see anyone at Mr. Ch'oe's, but then I find Mr. Ch'oe's nephew, who is taking a nap. Ah-ha—I had my breakfast after ten in the morning, meaning this is exactly the time for Mr. Ch'oe's nephew to take his nap.

I wake up Mr. Ch'oe's nephew and play a game of chess with him. I always beat him. For him, playing a game of chess with me is his ennui. The result is the same no matter how many times he plays. It is pointless for him to even try—but, if he doesn't play, what else is there for him to do when there's only two of us around?

And if losing is an ennui, then how can winning not be an ennui as well? I can play ten games with him, then win all ten games, and it is just as boring to lose all ten games. I cannot stand this boredom.

I will let him win just this once. I pretend to think really hard then place my pawn where I know is dangerous for me. Mr. Ch'oe's nephew yawns and makes his move. He knows he will lose, so he won't even pretend. This is his strategy: he wants to finish this game up as quickly as possible and lose again and again, so that the ever-victorious general—that would be me—will be overwhelmed by his own ennui and finally retreat. It is surely his plan to go back to napping once I leave.

Inevitably, I win again. He says he doesn't want to play anymore. I have no choice but to stop.

It is difficult to lose a game voluntarily. Why can't I be more like Mr. Ch'oe's nephew, who is utterly indifferent, now and always? Am I still beholden to this ir-relevant desire to win even as I suffocate in ennui? Is there no way to be a complete fool?

I hate this insignificant human desire that still remains within me more than anything else. I must find a way to elude this final thing. I must throw away my ability to recognize my ennui and be totally dejected.

2

I go to the village's creek. The draught has weakened its flow so much that I hear no sound of water. Why doesn't this skeletal stream of water cry out to me?

It is too hot. It is so hot that the leaves are all sagging and panting. The creek has no talent to sing out something cold in this heat.

I sit next to the stream. Ah—I think about what the title of my next rumination will be. But, of course, no title comes to my mind.

Well, then, I am not going to think about anything. Instead, I look over to the endless green fields, the horizon, and the clouds that cannot escape the cycle of trivial acrobatics of constant shape-shifting.

I assume 99 percent of the Earth is covered in this greenery of terror, meaning that the planet is in fact artless and dull colored. The color green is rare in my city. When I first arrived here in this countryside, I was amazed by this fresh greenness, and I fell in love with it. However, after five days had passed, I was shocked to discover that this endless green was in fact ugly and dry, a product of a god who was crude and tasteless in its making.

What is the world trying to do being so green? The color green does nothing all day. Like an imbecile, the green is so content with being green that it remains simply green.

When the night comes at last, the world surrenders its greenness to the abyss and sleeps soundlessly. Oh, sure, what great humility!

When the winter comes at last, all things initially lose their colors. However, the winter soon makes everything hideous in both shape and hue, and everything ends up looking like a shredded rag. I pity the farmers, who might as well be the greatest fools in the world, who must look at such wastelands all winter, while trying hard not to kill themselves.

Their lives, like these fields, are paint-washed in the monotonous color of ennui. When they work, the dullness will suffocate them like these hot, green fields. When they are not working, the dullness will be as rough and dirty as the winter wastelands.

Nothing excites the farmers. Even if lightning strikes their fields, to them it is nothing but a mere eventuality following thunder. Even if a tiger claims a village child, to them it is nothing but a form of divine punishment that occasionally happens in a mountain village like theirs. Really, in their fields, where there are no utility poles, what could they ever get excited about?

Steel-framed utility poles stand in a line over the back of P'albong Mountain, but not even a postcard gets wired to this village through their motionless power lines. I am certain electric current flows through them, but as long as the villagers' houses are lit darkly with lamps made out of pinewood, the poles may as well be indistinguishable from the *poplar* trees at the entrance of this village.

Do these villagers have hopes and dreams? I am sure they all hope for a good harvest in autumn. However, that is not hope. That is mere survival instinct.

Tomorrow. Tomorrow we will keep doing the same things we have been doing. Why are the endless tomorrows of ennui so endless? But the villagers here can't think about any of this. Even if such a suspicion were to come upon them like a flash of lightning, the hard labor of their days will put such thoughts to sleep immediately. Thus, how unfortunate are these farmers? Well, then—how happy am I to be conscious of my horrific ennui?

3

The cypress tree I see every day is languishing from the heat. From time to time, the water gets caught in a puddle and festers.

I am sitting near such a puddle. The water rots quietly before me.

A rooster idly crows during the day. Nothing is interesting about the rooster that crowed yesterday crowing again today. It does not matter if one listens to it or not. By some chance, my ears have caught his crowing, but I have nothing to say about it other than that I have heard it.

The rooster at least crows regularly at dawn and during the day, but the dogs of this village never bark. Are they all mute? No, I have evidence. When I, a stranger, threaten them and throw stones at them, they run away for miles and finally bark at me.

However, if I do not scare them and pass by quietly, then they just stare at me, a stranger who has come from far away. They do not bark, even though my face is pale and topped off by my wild, bird's nest–like hair. Truly strange. Why do these dogs never bark at me? In this world, there are many weird, humble, cowardly dogs.

If these cowardly dogs will not bark when they see me, then what will they ever bark at?

They have no reason to bark. Apparently, travelers do not come here. This village isn't even next to any main road; there is no reason for anyone to pass by this place. Sometimes, Mr. Kim visits, and he is from a neighboring village. However, he has the same complexion and speaks in the same dialect as Mr. Ch'oe, who is from this village. What reason is there for the dogs to bark at Mr. Kim? So, they never do. There are no thieves in this poor village. If thieves see how poor this village is, and if they have a shred of kindness in their hearts, then they will leave behind whatever dowry jewels they meant to steal from the poor women who live here. This village can be dangerous for thieves, for they can get their thieving hearts stolen from them.

What really is there for the dogs to ever bark at? For too long, probably since their birth, these dogs have given up their barking ways. I think the dogs of this village have not barked for a few generations, and they have lost their instinct.

Now, they might bark if they get hit by stones or sticks, and only if it hurts too much. However, humans can behave similarly; such change in nature probably should not be attributed to dogs only.

The dogs return to the gates of their owners' houses and sleep all day and night. Why? Because there is nothing for them to guard.

Mr. Kim's dog strolls up the street. Mr. Ch'oe's dog sees and rises to greet him. But even if they greet each other, there is nothing for them to do afterwards. They stand together for a while, then go their separate ways.

The dogs wag and prowl the village's streets. They prowl these streets day and night, but the dogs do not find anything to eat on these streets of dirt. All summer, the villagers eat barley and millet. Their side dishes are raw soybean paste and green chilis. Nothing is left in their kitchens. There is nothing left to be thrown out for the dogs to eat on the streets.

"Prowling has no benefit," the dogs think, "let's just take another nap." The dogs forget their natural gift for guarding things. They have been corrupted with their lust for naps—they have been corrupted so much that they should be cast out.

It's a sad business how these mute dogs have forgotten their barking. These lazy dogs do not know how to guard and protect. In the end, these idiot dogs are sacrificed to the villagers on Dog Day, and they are made into dog soups. The poor dogs don't even know how the lunar calendar works. They have no way of knowing when Dog Day is coming.

4

The newspapers do not get delivered to this village. Not even buses pass through here. How can I possibly get news about what's going on in the city?

Being here is the same as depriving all five of your senses. Underneath the stifling sky, stifling horizon, stifling landscape, stifling customs. The more I want to roll around, the more I remain stifled.

Is there any pain greater than being unable to think at all? Humans are able to think even when they are sick and bedridden. Actually, it is natural to think even more so in sickness. When the endless ennui suddenly strikes a person, their eyes open inward. They will be able to observe their inner self more closely, far more so than when they were too busy.

This excess of self-consciousness can be found in any modern person. It is what plagues them. It is a symptom of and the very definition of ennui. Physical inactivity and unavoidable ennui are the signs of self-consciousness at its peak excess.

But, as I am sitting beside the creek, I am locked out from even the excess of self-consciousness.

Even though I am lethargic, and even though I have an extreme case of ennui, my eyes hesitate opening inward.

I don't want to think anything. Until yesterday, thinking about dying was the only thing that entertained me. However, now, even that is tiresome. I will just sleep with my eyes open, and not think at all.

It is so hot. Why don't I take a bath? But the creek's water barely flows anymore, and it is rotting. It is just too much work to look for clean water—

And even if I do find clean water, I will not take a bath in it. I don't want to take off my clothes. No! It is despicable. I will not stand and allow my pale and brittle body to be spread out under the white sun to be dried.

What if my clothes are wet from my sweat? Let them stay wet.

So be it. But still, how can it be so hot? I return to my lodging and wash my face there. On my way back, as I am kicking the pebbles on the road, I come upon a pair of dogs fornicating. There is no artful technique in the sex of domesticated animals; it is just another manifestation of the ennui itself. The sex ritual of these dogs is not at all interesting to the village children nor to the country maids; I am certainly not interested in it either.

Back in my room, I look at the tin washbowl, reddish and blackened like the complexions of the villagers here. The bowl lost its original color long ago. I am guessing that the lady of the house brought it with her as a part of her wedding dowry. I wash my face in it, but even this water is warm. Even this water cannot withstand this summer heat. I finish cleaning my face, following the rules of face washing exactly.

Then, I take the remaining water in the bowl and go up to the fence of the house where the pumpkin vines are sagging. I find where the roots may be and pour the water there and hope that the vines will regain some of their vitality.

I dry my face with a towel smelling of sweat and sit on the porch. The innkeeper has four kids, and these children always copy what I am doing. They even use the same washbowl to wash their faces like I just did.

I initially think that they are washing themselves because it is hot, but that turns out not to be the case. Children are in their own ennui, and they are flustered from not knowing what to do, just like how I don't know what I am doing at all. They saw me washing my face, and decided to wash theirs, because I am not them, and that is all that is.

5

I despise how monkeys imitate human beings. What will end up happening to these children imitating me? We must not let these beautiful country children become monkeys.

I go back to the creek. The rotting water, the cypress tree, and nothing else. I sit there and look into the puddle of rotting water.

In that instant, I see something truly weird. Countless dirty specks arrange themselves and move toward a certain direction. They must be living beings. They must be minnows.

Not even in my dreams did I think that these lovely fish might be living in such a corrupted swamp.

They move rapidly within the puddle. They must be looking for something to eat. What do they eat to keep living? Bugs probably, but what is smaller than minnows?

They do not stay still. They all seem to have some sort of motive and move in formation. Motive! Indeed, even in the world of minnows there are urgent goals to be achieved.

Eventually, they come out of the puddle, and flow downstream like a mass of humanity. What are they planning? No, they may still turn around and come back upstream again. But for now, it is certain that they are going down. Down the stream, down the stream!

Five minutes pass. They have gone so far down the stream I can no longer see them. The puddle is quiet again, just like the rotting puddle I saw before the minnows.

I get up and decide to go to a meadow. There is a cow in the meadow.

I am excited that such a daring scene of minnows was hiding inside the rotting puddle. However, the phenomenon passed away like a sudden shower of rain as soon as I found it. I have no choice but to forget about it and let it go.

In the meadow, the cow's horns are no longer its weapons. The cow's horns are now merely one of the ingredients for making rims and temples of eyeglasses. The cow has been raised so that it can be beaten up by humans, thus it needs no weapon. The cow's horns are interesting only to a zoologist. In the days of its undomesticated wildness, the cow used to charge against its enemies with its horns—but now, the cow's present-day horns are an elegy to its former self, like the medals on a wounded soldier.

The cow's horns are more modest than the bull's horns. These elegiac horns have no business goring me. I lie down in the meadow next to it. I lie down and look at the cow.

The cow stops chewing the cud for a moment and looks at me.

The cow must be thinking, "Why is this human's face so pale? I guess he must be sick. I should be careful. He might endanger my life." I am certain the cow must have judged me in this way. But five minutes pass, and the cow goes back to its rumination. I let my mind ease up. I think I am more restful than the cow is right now.

The cow is the greatest being of ennui on Earth. It knows how to stay disinterested, so much so that it does not take joy from its appetite. How sick of the ennui does one have to be to be able to throw up the grass they just ate back into their mouth? How sick, indeed, to seem as though they take pleasure in that paradox, and chew on the sour and bitter taste of half-digested matter?

The bigger the cow, the greater and more sorrowful is its ennui. I lie in front of the cow. I try to be humble about my loneliness, which is as tiny as a germ compared to the cow's. I let myself think in secret and wonder whether or not I will be able to chew the cud of my contemplations.

6

I see about a half dozen children playing in the middle of a street. They appear as a gang of half-naked, bronze-skinned, and red-haired kids. Their murky countenances, sniveling noses, loincloths, and naked upper bodies make it impossible for me to tell what their sexes are.

If they are not girls, then are they boys? And if they are not boys, then are they girls? They seem about five to six years old. These children have chosen this street to have their fun.

The children pick up stones. There are no bricks or pieces of porcelain in this area. The villagers do not throw away broken dishes.

And then, they tear up wild grass. Wild grass—is this not the most common thing in the area? These children probably think anything green is already boring. But there is nothing else. They are banned from tearing up grain stalks, so wild grass will have to do.

They pulverize the grass with their stones. When the stone is dyed green, they throw away both the stone and the grass. They find and bring back fresh grass and fresh stones and repeat what they just did. For about ten minutes, they keep doing this again and again without saying a word.

And within those ten minutes, ennui comes for them. Grass is boring, and stones are boring. Is there anything else for them to do? No, nothing.

They all rise together. They have no sense of order, and there is nothing around here they can make something with to satisfy their impulses. They are all standing together because they simply got tired of sitting.

They lift their arms and look to the sky. They start yelling at the sky as if they are screaming. Then they jump up and down where they are standing. They jump and scream at the same time.

I start weeping as I watch this. How miserable does one have to be to play like this, to try to have fun like this? They don't know how to have fun. Their parents are so poor they cannot even buy toys for these beautiful children.

To my eyes, their jumping and screaming, with their arms desperately lifted toward the sky, do not seem fun at all. Why is the sky so blue today? And why will it be so blue tomorrow? Why are the mountain and the fields so green today? And why will they be so green tomorrow? The children's screams have to be curses thrown at the god who made everything blue and green.

The children cannot play with the dogs, because these dogs don't even know how to bark. Children cannot play with the chickens, because these chickens' eyes have turned red looking for food. The children's fathers and mothers are busy. Their older sisters and brothers are busy. The children have no choice but to be with other children. But what are they supposed to play with? They do not have a single toy, and they have run out of ideas for things to do. This is their misery.

Their playtime with stones and grass lasts five minutes. If they go on any longer then they will be too tired. Why do these innocents have to be tired? They eventually stop because they are bored of what they are doing.

They sit next to one another. They sit and make no sound. What are they doing? I don't know what kind of fun they are trying to have but it must be something— what kind of extraordinary entertainment have these small humans of ennui invented?

Five minutes pass, and they get up, one or two at a time, and stand aside. They have each pooped on their spots. Ah—this was their fun! This is their final creative fun when they have nothing left. But among them, one child does not get up for a while. His big poop just won't come out. He must be the ugly loser of this entertainment. I can see in the eyes of other children that they are going to ridicule him. O Creator! Give these children toys and some scenery!

7

The day darkens. The nights here are like the deep sea. I feel very weird.

I stay still and wonder why and realize that I must be hungry. Why am I hungry? What have I done to get this hungry?

A school of minnows was swimming inside a puddle that was corrupting itself. Perhaps there is another school of minnows stirring within my organs that I am unaware of. Whatever the reason may be, I have no choice but to eat.

As if in accordance with the law of inertia, on the dinner table are laid out pickled garlic, raw soybean paste, and green chilis boiled in soy sauce. When I eat them, each food feels different on my tongue. I have no way to explain why that is.

I eat out in the yard, and I can hear those numberless stars clamor above my head. What does that mean? To me the stars cannot be just a matter of astronomy. I also do not mean that they can be my poetic inspirations. They are in a state of eternal nirvana and have no fragrance or texture. It is a state of being which the absolute ennui cannot attain. Even the stars are so dull.

When I finish my dinner, I go out again. Above every rooftop I can see smoke drifting from little bonfires. Folks are sleeping in their yards, lying on their straw mats. They sleep while watching the stars. The stars, however, do not watch them. I know this because the folks go to sleep immediately when they lie down on their mats. They close their eyes and snore. The stars have nothing to do with them.

I walk back and forth on the street to quicken my digestion. Whenever I turn around to go back the way I came from, the number of sleepers increases.

How are they different have from common corpses? They are corpses that know how to eat and sleep—ah, I need to stop thinking so discourteously. I should go back and go to sleep.

I come back to my room and look around. My life is completely insulated from everything else—my life right now does not even have a trace of suicidal thought. It is the absolute of ennui. It is the ennui itself.

And yet, this thing called tomorrow exists. Even on a night like this, which seems as though it will never let the light back in, there is a thing called tomorrow waiting from beyond. Tomorrow is like a brutal local government official—I cannot escape this official. Tomorrow becomes today, and every day I have to suffer boredom; I suffocate, and my soul is stifled.

So how did I spend my time today? There is no reason to think about such things.

Let's just sleep! And while trying to sleep, perhaps unfortunately—or actually thankfully, I think about what I will do tomorrow. If I wake up again, I will play a few games of chess with Mr. Ch'oe's nephew, and I will try to go and see the minnows again at the puddle—I shall chew the cud of my few remaining memories like the cow, and I will enjoy this endless laziness.

A moth flies into my room and the light goes out. I cannot tell if it still lives because it is dark. I am guessing the moth suffered some burns, or else it is dead, but the moth knows how to survive. It knows enough to jump into the fire when it sees it—the moth is passion incarnate. It knows how to search restlessly for the fire.

But, where is my passion that seeks the fire, and where is the fire that is worthy enough for me to jump into? Nothing. There is nothing for me. My eyes have nothing, so they can only see nothing.

Darkness may be filling up my small room, or maybe it is filling up the whole universe—it doesn't matter. I am lying in the middle of it. I have nothing to breathe, nothing to touch, nothing that I want. I have nothing. But I am shuddering because I can sense that tomorrow is here. It is waiting on me like a servant next to my window. Its end is unknown.

May 4–11, 1937

AFTER SICKBED

He looked at the doctor's face many times. In his mind he was shouting to himself, "Doctors are people, too. They are no different than me!" However, he couldn't help but think that the doctor before him was a great magician, or a prophet. The doctor let go of his wrist. (Not moving a muscle) he became immeasurably disappointed. He didn't feel that the doctor had held his hand long enough. "Why did the doctor let go already? Why does he ever let go? Was he able to find out what is wrong with my ruined body just from my pulse?" He kept looking at the doctor as if he were a child looking at his grandfather's face after being yelled at, but the doctor's face was turned toward the door. There was a poster of the Ten Symbols of Longevity on the door. The doctor then turned again, raised his head, and stared at the ceiling as if he were deep in thought. Finally, the doctor sighed. He focused on the doctor's tightly closed mouth. It didn't seem like it was going to open, no matter how long he stared at it.

Later, he could hear people chatting in the living room, and his doctor's laughter was the loudest. This made him so resentful that he teared up, but he took comfort in the doctor's behavior as a sign that his illness wasn't serious. However, he could not forget the smell of alcohol on the doctor. He wondered, "Is it possible for doctors to diagnose illness correctly even when they are drunk?" He managed to calm himself and trusted his doctor (not against his own will, but because his faith in the doctor was so great). However, when the doctor's loud laughter from the main room reached his ears once again while he lay in his bed, he helplessly thought to himself, "Doctor, you don't take my illness seriously! You merely drunkenly played with my wrist. You acted as if you were in a deep thought, as if you were in a magic show! This is how worthless I am!" These thoughts turned into steel wires inside his head, and the wires wiggled out through orifices in his feverish head. He struggled alone. He was still able to hear the doctor declining a glass of wine in the main room: "Oh, please stop. I have work. I cannot drink so much." He could also distinguish the doctor's words from a shot glass clattering against something. His mind had not lost its cool completely yet.

It was a contradiction: though he believed in his doctor like he believed in God, he did not take his medicine at all. Whenever his nightly drug was warmed up and brought to him, his first thought was always, "I don't want it." His frowning brow, already filled with wrinkles, cracked more deeply at the sight of his drug. He looked at this yellow, syrupy medicine for a long time; apparently it was supposed to cure his chronic illness (he was now an excellent example of a chronically ill patient), but it was easier for him to believe in Jesus than to believe that the syrup could fix him.

His throat burned. His fever rose higher and higher into the night, and he lost consciousness, traveling between dream and reality. The right side of his chest boiled. If this boiling in his chest stopped, he thought he could survive. His chest pain (he assumed) was the reason why he lost consciousness.

"Who on this earth will understand my suffering? Who in the heaven?" He felt these ridiculous words forming inside himself. The medicine remained untouched beside him as he slipped into a coma. When he woke sometime later, he could observe large droplets of sweat rolling down his pale-yellow skin. His bodily functions stopped. With his eyes barely open, he looked at the clock hanging on his room's wall. When he finally got out of this incapacitation, ten minutes had passed, but to him it felt like he was coming back to his body after traveling for many years in foreign lands. When he picked up the medicine vial, it was as cool as icy water. "This is how worthless I am. My drug has gone cold, and no one ever came to tell me to drink it before it cooled." He drank the medicine in despair, but the medicine took away the thirst in his throat.

For a while, he was fully conscious. Under weak lamplight, he stared at his friend's painting leaning against the wall of his room. It depicted some troubling dream scenery. Usually, he could not look at the painting for too long (and only at night) because of how blinding it was, but now, his senses were numb. The memories of the last several months made him fall back into a coma. He once again traveled between dream and reality. In that confused state, he let his mind shake him awake. "I have always thought that this was my fundamental truth: though I had been a wretched beggar for a long time, I became a 'human' by casting out my lies to live truthfully. However, that was in fact not my truth. I found out that it was nothing but a ripple within a pathetic bug that lives only in his emotions. I once wrote incredible things about everything around me. It is only natural that I have forgotten what these things were about or even what kind of form they had."

For several months, he had lived in absolute despair (though it may not make any sense, it would be more fitting to say he "died" in absolute despair). When the moment came that he had no choice but to collapse onto his sickbed, he felt that "naturally, death has come for me." However, while he was lying in his bed for a day or two, as he was getting nearer to his biological death, his heart filled with burning hope and ambition. His consciousness recovered. He felt throttled by an energy that he hadn't tasted in a long time (and he was also pestered by it). Though his body became more and more emaciated, he was sure that his body was made of iron. It could never die.

On the night he collapsed (before then, he was simply lying down all the time, but that was the night he first began to lose consciousness), he had just received a long letter from one of his friends. It was not a well-written letter, but it was a transcription of his friend's sorrow. When he finished reading it, he felt a kind of terrifying, primal energy. While he was reading the letter, a dark cloud had tangled itself in his heart. "My mild-mannered friend offers me such truths, but all I have to offer him are my lies. How sad is this?" He then lay down on his stomach. His mind began to feel the pain that his body had been suffering. He could not bear it anymore. He took out some unused papers that had been stuck in between his other writings and began to write.

"Yes. I have lived deceitfully—and then I experienced a terrifying disturbance—I thought my lies were my foundation. I was a wretched beggar. I cast away my lies and resolved to live truly as a human being. I believed this. However, that was not my foundation either. I found out that it was nothing but an internal ripple within a pathetic bug who had lived only in his emotions. I realized that I could not help but live within the lie I had been living, for myself and for how I have interacted with everything around me until now ... so on and so forth."

While he laid down these sentences, he remembered how he had written a few verses of poetry as well. As his pen glided on the paper wearily, his consciousness got fuzzier, more dreamlike. He had no way of knowing now when and where he dropped his pen, and what the last thing he was writing was. The only thing he knew when he woke up again is that he lost consciousness while he was holding his pen.

A few days after the doctor's visit, after his anger toward the doctor had subsided, his consciousness began to have more moments of clarity, and he became human, burning with unknowable (baseless) hope. "If I can just rise..." He believed that he could pull Dante's *Divine Comedy* and Da Vinci's *Mona Lisa* right out of his mind effortlessly. He believed that he could not accomplish such feats because his body was still too weak. He took out his friend's long letter again and read it, and rather than a dark cloud, he could feel strong, boundless comradery with his friend. His eyes finally reached these words: "Mr. XX! Hope you will see the bright light one day!" Without realizing it, he started to cry out, "Oh, yes. I am seeing the bright light now!"

At a construction site in Ŭijut'ong
May 1939

SAD STORY

I have not been back here for a long time. Who told me to come here? I don't know. Much has changed. The elegance of the bridge here that I used to sketch is still palpable in the evening gloom; a small stream of water flows gently underneath its arch. The hills on both sides of the stream are well worn; waters have pooled inside their crevices like little ponds. The small rocks are like islands floating on the stream. They are spread out like simple furniture. If you follow the stream upwards, there is a wooden bridge where my friends and I took our graduation photo. The friends I knew then have all gone to live their separate lives, and I have no way of knowing where they are or how they are doing. I do not go any further up. Instead, I sit on a tree trunk short enough to be a stool and consider the water. I wonder if the twilight might come into the water where I see reflections of a leafless tree and a utility pole. The water flows over these reflections without hesitation. I do not touch the scenery in the water while it lies there. There is no wind this evening.

The lamp of the utility pole lights up inside the reflection as if to tell me that the night is coming. I turn around to see the actual pole rising above me. Its light comes into my eyes immediately. The pole might have drunk from a bottle of white liquor while I wasn't looking at it. Perhaps the night is really coming. The air is cold. Within the warm sleeves of my winter coat, my hands hold each other tightly and start sweating. My mind wanders the empty air, or perhaps it is sinking down into the water. Some of my limbs get lazy and forget to love. My hair, messy inside my hat, does not make any noise. I feel pity for my body's extremities. They all depend on my pathetic head to survive. If my body is a land, then it is a barren waste, and there is no strength left in my eyes, and my ears are filled with dust. Nothing can grow there. Sound still comes out of my throat, but it is like the sound of an old harmonium. My nose is filthy; its nostrils have been replastered numerous times. For nearly twenty years, these limbs have trusted my head, and have followed its cruel lead. While the head itself, ignoring their profound loyalty, is now trying to be ruined.

The family of the body—hands, nose, ears, feet, waist, calves, neck, and others—must have figured out what their master is planning to do. They stand aside, look at one another worriedly, but still depend on one another, and wait for the inevitable. Meanwhile, the night gets darker. The stars gather one by one. They are greeting one another: "Good evening, where do you come from?" And stories begin to sprout among them. There is a star smoking a fancy cigarette. Another star cleans his glasses with a handkerchief. There are also stars taking a commemorative picture together. I am no longer looking up; instead I gaze into this party hall of stars by looking at its reflection on the water. The time is near. Tonight's program is filled with a variety of entertainments. I hear the golden-buttoned footmen going around and closing the windows of the hall. The party hall suddenly grows dark, and every star's face is full of life. Their lips shake with excitement, and some of them smile meaningfully at one another, blinking their eyes. Andromeda, Orion—they all take their seats. One of them even takes out their cigarette and lights it.

Suddenly, someone hurriedly comes in from the back of the hall. All the stars tilt their heads in unison toward the noise. Their troubled hearts perform acrobatics, and their breathless show hides their light, deepening and darkening their party, the receding night sky. "What is going on?" someone says. Then, a deep and soft voice is heard from beyond the wide sky and says the following liquid words like music: "Everyone, a messenger has come to tell you to return here early this evening." The stars all stand up at once. A black velour hat looks great on one of the stars, and a Western-style cloak fits magnificently on the shoulders of another star. Their enamel heels on the soft carpeting of the hall make grating, twisting noises. The stars scatter as they walk out. The hall is now nearly empty, and a few lamps are still on, but an old, night-shift janitor comes in and turns off the remaining lights. Within minutes, all the lights are out, and only the spit-out chewing gum and peeled-off caramel wrappers remain, scattered on the stiflingly dark sky.

What happened? Perhaps there was a death at the royal palace. I cross my arms and massage my cowpox vaccination scar near the shoulder of my arm. My mother and father are both covered in smallpox scars. They are kind people. My father only has seven fingers. He lost three fingers while working at the printing press of the royal court. My mother does not know her birthday, nor her name. She never had a family of her own. I am quite jealous of anyone who has in-laws, but my father is not jealous of any man who has a mother-in-law. I have never given my parents money. I have never bought them candy. I have never bowed to them. When they gifted me a pair of unoiled shoes, I wore them and went to an alley they know nothing about and ruined those shoes. When they paid for my school's monthly tuition, I specifically studied words they could never read. And yet, my parents never once scolded me. After I stopped sucking on my mother's tits, I left them for twenty-three years, and when I came back, they were still poor. When I returned, my mother took my worn cloth belt and folded it. My father put a nail on a wall of their tiny house, so I could hang my coat and hat. My younger siblings had all grown up, and my little sister was now a young woman. But I still do not know how to make money. How do you make money? I don't know how. I don't know.

My friends are all gone, too. I have no adults in my life. I don't have any manners. I am not a man of perseverance. My hands caress my cheek. They are as cold as a stranger's hands. My hands seem to say, "What are you thinking about so deeply, when you have become so thin?" My hands must have realized that my head has decided on ruin. Other usual consolations follow. All useless. Nothing will come of them. My mind has already thrown out my stories in secret. They were my final property. A small bag of medicine and a small bowl of water are all that remain. One day, or one night, when the rest of you are in deep slumber, I will ruin myself, just a little bit. That is the only thought I have written down. I will not tell my mother, nor my father. I will not call my friends. I will be ruined like an orphan.

Hilariously, it begins to rain. The gentle ripples on the water are dizzying. The raindrops make no sound, like rubber shoes. They are quieter than tears. The air gets cold. I see a magpie, and I wonder if its nest will be able to repel this invasive rain. The times have gotten tough for the magpies. They have nearly disappeared from Seoul. On a long, rainy night like this, a vast number of people must be crying. An unusually bright light pours out of the window of a Western-style house across the way from me, but someone inside closes the window immediately. A warm room is closing its eyes to have some idle fun. Let it have its fun. However, this spot is so cold, and the rain gets heavier. The rain comes. The rain is coming. Once the rain stops, the day will get suddenly very cold. My worries about the season make me anxious, which in turn makes me long for people. My lady has been standing right next to me, and she hasn't said a word. She is like a mute. I look at her face closely, and it is white and delicate. In that dark night, she is clear and clean like a pocket watch. She must have danced awhile under the moonlight a long time ago, but there is no spot that I can kiss on her face. For any spot on a face to be kissable, it must be a small, vacant space that serves no purpose. However, on my lover's face, there is not a single empty space. I am in the process of placing this lady quietly inside my heart. She makes no sound, even when her mechanical spring is completely wound up. When my emptied head is ruined, I will do so while I am choking on this *Simone* of mine. This lady is the lost title of my mind, and she is the nail on which I hang my mind before I throw it out. Every other limb stays silent about my head's vanity. Lover, I will not place a finger on your body. Let us die. Is this going to be a double platonic suicide? No, this is going to be two separate suicides. I take out my notebook and open it. Today is November 16, and December 1 is two Sundays from now. In two weeks, then. Yes, truly. The lady's face is as white as a paper window. A crack appears on it, through which she laughs. The lady writes her pledge on my notebook. Her words look like musical notations. She signs it with the print of her thumb: "We will die together. There won't be any mistake." Yes, I am so thankful. I can hear the song I love the most in my mind, and I begin to whistle. I decide to forget about all the things I am sorry about in the world, and I wave my clean handkerchief like a white flag to commemorate my defeat. "Where are those cars going in this rain? Yes." Beyond the hill there is the market of the Holy Mother. "I hear there is something priced for one *won*, and now I want to burn it all down." Why? The cars splash water on their headlights, and swarm over the hill. On a night like tonight, when the air is humid, I need to powder myself a little bit more and use a stronger fragrance. It is very humid. The rain rains down even heavier than before. My coat is thoroughly wet, and now my pants are getting wet, too. No one is looking. There is nothing to be ashamed about. If I meet anyone, then I will be ashamed for them. However, they will not know why I am ashamed. The demon who lives inside me is tiny. He looks like someone who has struggled all his life. He weighs next to nothing. The demon is back after having won a great fortune. He takes off his gloves and briefly looks at his gaunt but cheerful face in the mirror. Afterwards, he paints scenery on a clean canvas. He only uses one color.

It is the scene of a port I once visited. The day is grey there. The food there is not good. A young man puts a letter into a mailbox while a young woman stands by his side. The darkness swells with the waves. I worry about the cold, red rain splashing into the mailbox and wetting all the letters within. The young man smacks his lips and walks toward the pier together with the woman. What time is it, four o'clock? The sun busily descends westward, and the dreary wind blows in with the scent of the rising tide in its embrace. "Give me five packs of cigarettes and a chocolate for fifty jeon." Dear, look at this, it's like a spool without any empty space inside it. "Farewell." The alleyway is long, and skins of tangerines are scattered throughout its paved path. Then, the tooting of a horn—it is the sound of a steam whistle from the pier. This tooting must be painted with light purple. Let's go to the pier. Ah, they have a bus here, too. Today, the flags on the top of the ship's mast are in commotion, gasping for breath. The young man unbuttons the second button of his shirt. Are you not worried someone might assassinate you? The harbor's water is as dark as marujeng ink. A block of wood floats on the water. From which part of me did that one come out? Ah, a seagull is flying. The seagull is wearing raggedy clothes today. The path in the air must also be thick with clouds today. Here, let's get on. The side of the ship is dark and lots of oysters are attached to it. Anyways, let's get on now. It must be time. More tooting of the horn. We must be leaving. I am going to lie down for a bit. "I will, too." I have to look out through a round porthole window. The lights have come on on the port. I touch the forehead of my lover. It is warm. It is boiling. What can be done? Please don't. I light up a cigarette. I smoke one, and then I smoke two, then three, and then four, and then five. I end up trying to smoke fifty cigarettes, and during this time one must make the choice. Dear, while I am doing this, why don't you have a chocolate? The lights come on inside the cabins of the ship. Everyone must be tired. Forty, forty-one cigarettes. Soon enough, I smoke forty-nine cigarettes. How my tongue aches! The early evening staggers. Dear, look at all these rows of cigarette stumps! There are forty-nine now. Wake up. Let's go up to the deck. The woman quietly stands up, but she says nothing. It is cloudy. The sea is dark without the stars, as if it has shut its door. My lover's skirt flutters in the salty wind. I light up the one remaining cigarette, and while it is burning away, I make my final decision. Dear, are you not sad? The woman shakes her head. It is now all burned. Close the door. The sound we make jumping off the ship is smooth, then there is the sound of a struggle, pushing against the suffocating darkness of the night, and finally the loud sound of the sea breaking. Goodbye. The demon slowly signs his name on the corner of this painting.

Two weeks pass by helplessly, and the holiday finally arrives. I am walking with the lady by the sandy shores of a river. I cough. I cough and cough. I am down with a sudden cold. The wind mercilessly blows on the river against its stream. My pocket is filled with my worrying. The lady seems much shorter than usual. She has no vitality. I knew this was going to happen. You are too young. My worrying grows next to such a young body. The promised day continues to be pushed back. Merchant vessels follow one another as they go up the river; their sails are full of all the wind they've eaten. Why don't you sing a song? The sky is cold, and the ground is wet. The woman's weight is lighter than a snack. I turn around and barely manage to light up a cigarette and breathe as well as I can. I cough again. Let's go over there. There is a wall of trees, planted there to act as a windbreak, and amidst them there is a railroad. Not a single magpie lives here, and the leaves have fallen so much. There is no other place as desolate as this. I walk arm in arm with the lady, stepping on muddy, slushy leaves. We walk east. A train passes us by, transporting gravel, and it whistles. We stand there and witness the scenery that looks like it came straight out of a children's fairy tale. Occasionally, a path appears out of the fallen leaves, but we never meet anyone else. As far as I can tell, we are in desolation, which exists beyond the border of humanity. I massage the woman's low shoulders and pronounce softly into her roselike ear. Let's go home. "No, I have left my home forever today." Let's wait five more days. "I will wait, but do you have to die?" Of course. "Let's say you are dead, why don't you let me borrow that soul of yours?" I can't. "Even if I promise to die anytime as a security?" No.

How can this be? I take out a letter from my pocket and rip its pages apart on the spot. I had written the letter to my dearest friend. It said, "When you receive this, me and my love will no longer be of this world." But, what of it? I have no courage to take my one life, the only thing that I own. I have not cultivated myself enough. Still, I will try to do my best. Suddenly, black-and-white ribbons one wears at funerals are all over this deep forest, where no magpies visit. The lady's face turns pale.

———————

June 1937

A LETTER TO MY SISTER

You and your lover told me that he would be leaving on an early August train the next night, but both of you left on the train the next morning.

Though I am hardly the person to act as the elder in our family, I am still older than both of you.

You might have told me, "We cannot live apart from each other," which could have been a way of telling me what you needed. I certainly would not have said,

"I cannot allow it."

In fact, I may have helped you both to get away from our mother and father; that much I am able to do.

The fact that you still did it on your own without telling me, your older brother, who hopes for nothing else but your happiness, has given me much grief.

You and K came to me one morning, to let me know that K would be leaving on a northbound train as scheduled. The day before the train's departure the two of you came to me to discuss your plans, and we agreed that K would go alone, and you and me would go to the station to say farewell. Don't you think that would have been proper?

How could you have said to me then, without a hint of worry on your face, "Well, then, dear brother, we will see you at the station tomorrow."

"Sure! I will be there. See you again soon."

And that was how we parted ways. That ended up being my farewell to you and K. That is how you both had planned to say goodbye to me.

Because I am such a stubborn and slow person, I still went to the station that early August night, right on time, when the train was supposed to leave. But I finally began to worry a little and thought, "These little kids must have lied shamelessly. They must have planned something behind my back!"

Of course, as it turned out, when the train workers started to check for tickets, you were nowhere to be seen.

"Is this what I think it is—" was what I first thought, but I stayed and waited for you until the station closed. Even when the last train left, you could not be found. I left the station alone, but even then I thought, "Perhaps there was a problem at the laundromat with K's suit, and that is why they could not make it to the station on time. Whatever happened, they will reach out to me soon enough." And so, I waited.

You would have let me know if you could not make it to the station on time, but all was quiet. I laughed nervously to myself and hesitated. Some friends of mine came back from Tokyo that night, and I ended up drinking with them all night.

Dear sister, a wire arrived instead of your apologetic face, and it wasn't even your words. K's words alone let me know that you were with him, telling me not to worry.

When I got the wire, I could not help but smile. I am happy for the two of you and think highly of your bravery. You cut me like a blade slicing water.

Dear Ok-hŭi! Please, don't you ever feel I would be angry with you!

But, do beg for forgiveness from our mother and father who have lost you so suddenly, like lightning striking out of the blue.

I should also leave home myself, following your example. In the past twelve years, after graduating from school at age sixteen, I still haven't let go of that futile dream of mine.

Your other brother has gone somewhere again and has not returned.

You have crossed the border. You are now in a foreign land.

The three of us siblings are all undutiful children who lack filial piety.

However, none of us think that this is wrong.

We must go and come back. We must go even if we never come back.

You have done the right thing for yourself and for your lover. For twelve years, I have agonized over doing it myself, but perhaps I was held back by the grace of being adopted as someone else's firstborn, or perhaps it was because I do not amount to anything. Whatever the case may be, I stay here, caught in the ebb and flow of humiliation. I am ashamed.

I gave you my consent for your romantic relationship with K, and I was the only one to do so in our family. Though K is a good person, I know well how his lot in life has been unfortunate. Thankfully, K was born to a family he does not have to worry about. He only needs to worry about feeding himself. And yet, I can tell that he isn't the kind of person who will be satisfied with simply feeding himself.

K has told me about what his dreams are, and I do not criticize them. It is certainly one way of living a life. It is no different than any other way of escaping humiliation, and in that regard, I must accept his choice.

In fact, I supported him when he confessed to me that he will leave his family, even though he was another's adopted firstborn like myself.

Though I may end up being food for crows on the wild wastes, I also want to live for my dream as well. So, I told K, as if I were suggesting it to him, that he should indeed go abroad and live for three years.

Three years—I thought three years seemed like too long a time for two people to be longing for each other. So, I asked him, what will you do with Ok-hǔi when you leave? And I—

The two of you had been seeing each other for nearly a year at that point. I assumed you both knew each other well. Even if K had been a high-ranking minister of the court, that would not have mattered if he did not catch your fancy. He did catch it. So, I really had no say in this matter, telling you and him what to do with my ridiculous mouth, and yet—

Because I wanted to suggest a few things, because I could not stay silent as your kin—

I told K that three years is indeed a long time, and advised him that after his first year there, after he was well settled, he should come back and marry you and have a wedding, but I did not want it to be a wedding for a wedding's sake. I think any kind of wedding is ridiculous, but we have our mother and father to think about, and what people will think of the two of you, because I do not want you to be ridiculed by others for not doing such a small thing—

And that's about all I said to K, and I asked both of you what your intentions were. K told me that he would do what I suggested and come back next spring and marry you, then take you with him. However, what you initially told me was different. You said that it didn't matter if you had a wedding or not, and that you would go with him right away. You said that you would live together as long as you are alive and die together when you must die. You could not wait for him with your mouth hanging open—to come back and take you with him, while not knowing what might happen to him in a distant land. Also, you said, you couldn't wholly trust a man's heart—and finally, you resolved that you should have some struggle in your own life, because you had lived a sheltered life like that of a frog in a well.

The structure of our society is still male oriented. When the times are good for a man, it is good to have a woman to share those pleasures. But, when the times are hard, a woman can easily end up being the rope that binds her man. I told you again that you should let K settle down first and make sure he can provide for you on his own before coming back for you. At the time, you had no choice but to agree with me, and gave me an OK sign with your hand. With K right in front of you and me during that meeting, I made sure to get as many promises I can from him—

But now I know. My advice could not get in between the love you and K have for each other. There was not even a paper-thin crack for my advice to slide through. And yet, I cannot help but feel assured before such love.

As the youngest of three siblings, you acted like a baby for a long time and were the last to grow up. I was the earliest. During your school years, the only time you ever left our neighborhood was when the teachers led you on a field trip to another city. And now, to think that you are going to be crossing the border shakes me awake at night.

I have always thought of you as a child. When did you grow up so fast, into such an incredible adult? The time has come when parents can no longer treat their daughters as they were once treated. Older brothers, too, will get easily fooled if they treat their little sisters as if the sisters were vain and had nothing to show for themselves. At least, that is how I feel.

Though I still get dizzy as if my head has been struck by a hammer, I think about the reason why you had to leave our home.

First, you must have thought that you had to possess your lover totally, and since this isn't something human beings can change about themselves, there really was no other way to go about it.

Second, our parents did not consent to the two of you dating. When their children's romantic relationships are fair, then the parents must not only consent to it but have the duty to guide that relationship in a better direction—

Unfortunately, our mother and father are too old and do not know how to do such things. And you did not have the heart to try persuading them. You could only show it to them through your actions.

Third, while it is not yet clear, you are aware of what making a living on your own entails. It never sat well with our parents that a woman might be able to get a job and become economically independent. Our parents would say, "It is fine to earn some money, but a girl's body might get easily ruined doing so."

Once, when you could not find a job in Seoul no matter how much you tried, you wrote a letter to one of your friends, who was working at a factory in Gyeongdo. You planned to become a factory worker yourself. Our family is so poor that we cannot even afford to buy new socks for you. This is a shameful thing for me, as your older brother—but, I am thankful that you never resented me.

That is the kind of person you are. You will never be a rope that binds K, and you will do your own thing, and help K as well.

So, you have left. Now that you have left, do not worry about your family, and put all your heart into your shameless success. It may take more than three years. It may even take ten years. Even if you are defeated and end up being food for carrion on a naked wasteland, do not think to set your feet on home soil again unless you succeed.

I think I shall leave our home, too. At least once. I know that I must guard this soil of ours, but I also know that a duty of protecting is different from the duty of leaving. It is more desperate. You have left, your other brother has left, and if I leave, then who shall protect our aging parents? Do not worry. That is my job as the first-born, and I will figure something out. If nothing works out, an unfortunate past will have been sacrificed for a brilliant future.

The night you and K were crossing the border, I was listening to the reports about the Olympics while drinking with friends. Our people must not go on rotting like this. We must be able to stand together with all the other people in the world proudly and live as brilliantly as we may. You must wake up!

In the slums of Odong Tree Valley, underneath the Shindang-ri Ridge, your grandmother, who is nearly a corpse, and your father, who cannot move freely, and your mother, who has shriveled after fifty years of manual labor, are still alive. When they got your wire, they wept. Every day, you used to come all the way there to say hello to us and eat with us. Now, who shall come and see us?

Mother said, "I have lost my horse. How shall I live with this empty feeling by my side?"

Since then, I drag myself around wearing my worn-out shoes and act as her horse.

Our parents, who don't know how to criticize anyone or anything, wept like rain simply because you had disappeared. I said to them, "What is all this noise? It isn't like she is dead!"

And with all that yelling, I somehow managed to calm them down, but I too began to miss you when I realized that I won't be able to see you for at least three years. You feel the love you always had for your siblings only after you have been separated from them.

I shall study for three years, too. And I will escape the humiliation of this abnormal life. When that happens, let us meet again with brighter, livelier faces.

No matter what, please return home as soon as possible once you succeed in the way you hope for.

Of course, because you are a woman, you were bound to leave our home at one point for another man's house, so this whole event has only made what was bound to happen happen much sooner than expected. It has certainly surprised our parents, but I am fine.

Anyways, because of what you have done, I have understood much about myself. I will wake up, too.

I am worried that your slight frame will have a tough time withstanding the severe northern weather. Never forget to take care of yourself. For poor people like us, our body is the one and only possession we have. It is our last belonging.

Please write to me.

Even if the whole world turns against you, remember that I am always on your side. The world is wide. There will be many things that will surprise you, and there will be many things that you will learn.

Once this letter gets published in *Jungang* magazine, I will send you a copy. Please read it with K, and please remember your older brother's words.

I bless you.

Dear Ok-hŭi, remember how you used to model for me for spare change when I still dreamed of being a painter? Dear Ok-hŭi, do you know you are the only one who understands your debauched brother, who always fails to uphold filial piety? Dear Ok-hŭi, you have suddenly grown up, and you now live in a distant land with your lover. I bless your future.

This took me two days to write. I understand it might be hard to figure out why I wrote this at all, but I am publishing this in a magazine, hoping that other older brothers who have sisters like you will read this, too. Please remember my loyalty to you.

On the fifth morning,

Your loving brother

September 1936

TOKYO

Before I saw the real Marunouchi Building, nicknamed Marubiru, it was at least four times bigger and far more amazing in my mind. Will I also be disillusioned like this when I see New York's Broadway? Anyways, my first impression of Tokyo: "This city reeks of *gasoline!*"

People with barely functioning lungs like myself have no right to live in this city. The smell of gasoline seeps into my body though I keep my mouth closed; I taste it whenever I try to eat something. The citizens of Tokyo will all eventually smell like automobiles.

No one lives around the Marunouchi Building except other buildings. Automobiles are pedestrians' shoes. The few who force themselves to walk in this city are the holy philosophers, contemptuously glaring at capitalism and the ending of a century. Everybody else simply puts on their automobiles to go out for a walk.

Ridiculously enough, I had already walked in this neighborhood for five minutes when I wised up and got a taxi—inside the taxi, I studied the title of the twentieth century. The moat of the imperial palace passed outside the taxi's window, and innumerable automobiles busily tried to maintain the twentieth century's profitability. My personal ethos smells of the stale nineteenth century, and it is a very dignified thing: it cannot comprehend how there can be so many automobiles.

Shinjuku is very much a Shinjuku. Luxury is on thin ice there. At Huranseu Yasikki, my companions and I drank coffee with milk already added in, but I felt like I was paying a bit more than I should have, like paying ten jeon for a cup of coffee when I should only be paying nine jeon and five ri.

Eruteru.[1] The people of Tokyo write France as "Huransu." My memory tells me that Werther is the name of the person who had the juiciest romance in the world, but Eruteru does not sound as sorrowful as Werther.

Shinjuku—three districts that have prospered like demon flame—beyond its vicinity there is a wooden fence and unsold land and signs that say DO NOT URINATE. Still, I am sure there are some houses, too.

Though I needed more sleep, Mr. C guided me to Tsukiji Little Theater. The theater was closed when we got there. It was the birthplace of Japan's New Theater movement. There were many different posters on the walls, but to my eyes the theater looked like a badly built café. Even though I missed out on cheap movies, I returned to this theater a few times afterwards, which, I think, makes me a theater lover of the highest quality.

Mr. C argued that "Theater is more entertaining than life itself." Whereas Mr. H remained skeptical. Mr. H's rent changed all the time like the feathers of a mountain dove: sixteen yen for winter, fourteen yen for summer, and fifteen yen for spring and autumn. This in turn made him more cynical, and he often mocked himself. Because I am very forgetful, I asked if I could get a room that did not trick one with rents that changed their prices every season. As an answer, my landlord's servant girl consoled me by telling me that I must be smarter than I look, since a country boy like me has managed to come alone all the way to Tokyo. In turn, I consoled the girl by telling her that the wart hanging on the left hillside of her nose symbolizes happiness. Additionally, I let her know that there was nothing I wished for more than to have a clear view of Mount Fuji from my apartment.

The day after, at seven o'clock, there was an earthquake. I opened my window and watched great Tokyo shudder, filled with yellow lights. The servant girl encouraged me to look at Mount Fuji beyond the city at that moment as it reared its grey-haired head, which stood there like a children's cookie underneath a clear sky.

The Ginza was an introductory text for illusions. If one does not walk its streets, one might as well lose their voting rights. They say when women buy new shoes, they must walk on the pavements of the Ginza before they get inside an automobile.

The Ginza of daytime is the skeleton of Ginza of nighttime, which is Ginza without "the." The Ginza of daytime is ugly. Like furnace pokers, the twisted steel frames form the curvy neon sign of Salon Haru. The sign is as shabby as the wavy perm of a working girl who has just finished her shift. However, the city hall has posted signs: "Do not spit on the streets." So, I have no choice but to swallow mine.

The eight districts of the Ginza, according to my estimate, should just be two districts. Why? I could meet a rich girl with wild hair dyed red twice in half an hour, because she would have come out to enjoy the most beautiful time of the day. As for me, this joyless and dry promenade was nothing more than a cow's rumination. I went to an underground public toilet by a bridge, and while excreting, I recited all the names of my friends who bragged about visiting Tokyo.

Shiwatsu—means the twelfth month of the lunar calendar. In the corners of the Ginza, Salvation Army's kettle pots are set up like gun rests for infantry rifles. One jeon. One jeon can get someone enough gas to boil up a bowl of soup. However, I cannot throw away valuable money into their kettle pots. Anything they might say in gratitude does not benefit my life any more than one jeon worth of gas. Their gratitude could ruin my nice walk. Thus, when modern boys and girls coldly pass by the kettle pots, they are not being unreasonable. A young girl in the Salvation Army uniform, whose only flaw was some pimples on her face, was filled to the brim with her youthful attractiveness. I wanted to urge her to change her mind and tell her, "You can join the Salvation Army after menopause!"

These days, the seven-floored buildings of Mitsukoshi, Matsuzakaya, Itoya, Shirokiya, and Matsuya no longer sleep at night. However, we are not to go in there.

Why? Their insides do not have seven floors. It is all one floor, and there are so many goods and countless shopgirls that it is too easy to get lost in there.

Bargains, deals, sales, which one will we ever pick? Whatever we end up doing, those words can't even be found in a dictionary. There is nothing cheaper than bargains, deals, or sales. And jewels or furs are not supposed to be "cheap," so these smart advertisements understand very well the type of customers who would never consider buying anything "cheap."

When night comes, Ginza without "the" finally appears. The tea at Korombang Café and the books at Kinokuniya bookstore are what pass for refined culture in Tokyo. However, people who are even more refined go to the café Beuraeuzil and have a straight shot of espresso. The waitresses are all dressed in uniforms with patterns of autumn leaves, but to my eyes those leaf shapes look like germs of venereal diseases. In Brazil, I heard that the trains do not use coal, but use coffee beans as fuel instead. Here in Tokyo I try to swallow as much coal as I can, but my passion doesn't catch fire.

After an *ad balloon* lands at night, the sky of Ginza should be filling up with sparkling stars according to the will of God, but the last descendants of Cain have forgotten the stars a long time ago. The citizens of Ginza have been taught to fear the poisonous gas more than Noah's flood, and naively take the subway instead of walking home. O dear Moon, Li Bai once composed verses about you! How much better would it have been if you had also shared the fate of the nineteenth century?

———

May 1939

1. Yi Sang is mimicking Japanese pronunciation of Werther, the name of the main character in Goethe's *Sorrows of Young Werther*.

Stories

translated from the Korean by

DON MEE CHOI
and **JOYELLE
MCSWEENEY**

YI SANG'S HOUSE

DON MEE CHOI

In December of 2016, I was able to spend a month in Seoul on a translation residency funded by the Literature Translation Institute of Korea. I stayed in downtown Seoul, next to the Gwanghwamun Square and the beautiful Gyeongbokgung and Changdeokgung palaces I used to run around in with my siblings when I was a child. I was also within walking distance of Yi Sang's House. Yi Sang, trained as an architect, was an influential avant-garde poet and writer. He lived here from age one to twenty-three, raised by his well-off uncle and aunt. The building itself is not the original structure, but this site was where his uncle's house used to stand. I thought the design of the house beautifully mirrored the interiority of Yi Sang's and his protagonists' psyche—his protagonists are often idle, penniless, tuberculosis-ridden artists, holed up in dark rooms. Yi Sang himself died from TB at the young age of twenty-seven, in Tokyo.

As you walk through the front glass door, you see a dark, metal door that opens up to an almost pitch-dark chamber. Poet Kim Hyesoon, who accompanied me to Yi Sang's House, pointed out that this dark space used to be an attic. In traditional Korean houses, in the main room of the house where guests are also received, there is a sliding paper door that opens up to an attic. Traditionally, the main room was where men sat and performed their scholarly duties, but who knows what they really did while women toiled away, cleaning up after their mess. It could be thought of as a living room, but, for my family, it turned into a bedroom at night. The attic is an ideal space for any child. I spent many hours gazing down at our tiny courtyard from the attic window because everyone and everything looked so different from that vantage point. During summers, I pressed my tummy against the cool, bare floor of the attic and read for hours, trying to forget about the heat.

Inside the attic chamber, slides of Yi Sang's work, including his drawings, were projected onto a wall. Experimentalist Yi Sang and his contemporaries were strongly influenced by European modernism, particularly Dadaism and surrealism, which came to be introduced in Korea mostly through Japanese translation during the occupation (1910–1945). One of his protagonists, who is Yi Sang himself, mentions Cocteau and says that he used to order postcards from the International Modern Art Exhibitions held in Tokyo.

In both of the short stories, "Spider&SpiderMeetPigs" and "True Story—Lost Flower," Yi Sang utilizes Korean transliteration of English and French words, which was thought to be a radical thing to do at the time. But writing and publishing in Korean was even more of a radical thing. Writing and publishing in Korean signaled a political opposition, a literary resistance to the Japanese colonial rule. I was initially introduced to Yi Sang's stories through my father's love of his stories. He told me several times that he read Yi Sang late into the night in order to forget about his hunger, that Yi Sang's stories helped him through his bleak childhood. Yi Sang's stories are bleak too, yet there is also much humor and satire in them through self-mockery. My father must have identified with Yi Sang's helpless, emaciated, hungry, male artist figures who somehow managed to get through another drab day.

As the resented child of a second marriage, my father was shunned, ill-fed, and made to sleep in the maid's room. A fairy tale, indeed. While the maid darned a sock placed over a light bulb, my father read books in Japanese. To keep reading late into the night, he had to translate to her what he was reading. And to avoid the nuisance and difficulty of translating, he offered her just brief synopses and told her that he could tell her more only if he kept on reading. For me, translation began with translating for my mother in Hong Kong. I dreaded it. I dreaded exposing my inadequacies, my failures in language. Translation for me then was, and it still is to some degree, a painfully repetitive journey of farewell and return, between home and elsewhere, between Korean and my frayed English. Only much later, I learned that cultural imperialism uses language to produce failure, inferiority. As a child from a neocolony of the US, I had already failed even before I set foot onto the British colony. Unlike my father, I didn't know how to cheat my way out of translation. I could only mumble and sulk.

For Yi Sang and my father, Japanese was their colonial language as English is a colonial language for me. We did not choose it; it chose us, historically, and that's the nature of a colonial language. It finds you. It can even track you down via the US Terminal High Altitude Area Defense anti-missile system and make a foreigner out of you in your own country, which is to say, your home is no longer your home. How else could you explain a golf course instantly turning into a military installation site for THAAD? (A fairy tale, indeed.) And you remain as a colonial subject within or without. Hence, the most poignant thing I noticed while translating Yi Sang was how his protagonists were coping with their homesickness in Tokyo as well as at home in Seoul. Yi Sang's use of foreign words signals homesickness, a state of perpetual colonial exile. I am self-trained, but well trained, nevertheless, in detecting homesickness. I rely on my attic vantage point when translating. And translation is a coping mechanism for homesickness, my wings of return.

I also know how to detect dread, fairy-tale dread. Yi Sang's stories are essentially colonial fairy tales. In "Spider&SpiderMeetPigs," a husband and wife are spiders, living in a room "as tiny as a satsuma orange box" filled with spider stench and garbage. We know that they are fairy-tale spiders by the fact that spider husband despises household goods. Any average spider would revel in spinning its cobwebs amidst household clutter. And his wife is also a fairy-tale spider in her own right—her socks change seasonally and she jumps at any chance of buying new clothes despite getting tossed out and bruised by humanity. "Spider and spider, spider and spider? Sucking on each other?" Spider husband, hopelessly weak from TB, lives off his spider wife, a barmaid who entertains and lends her scrawny body to pigs, colonial capitalist investors. Spider husband dreads leaving his room. He dreads the outside world. When he goes out, he suffocates from "wall after wall stuck to the buildings" and "all the shut windows"—the new modern space that has emerged under the occupation. By rule, colonial space is a confined, compressed space. That's how human, natural, financial resources are extracted and exploited. "Asifconversingwithsomeonehegesturedwithhisarmsandcircleda-roundthepaperthinwallsofAInvestmentswonderingwhat'sinside." Hence, Yi Sang's sentences are also compressed, deprived of air, barely leaving any gaps between words, syllabically speaking. And if there is any hint of air, it's "noordinaryair." These syllabic silks are spun within the spider couple's claustrophobic fruit box–like room, and the silks extend all the way out to investment offices. The office walls are covered in graph paper like cobwebs, "paintedupanddownwithredand-bluelines." How would a pair of scrawny husband and wife spiders survive and resist under the colonial rule if not for silk language? Yi Sang's silk language is essentially a fairy-tale language under a particular fairy-tale condition, which still persists today, more or less, under a different imperial domination that overpowers even the former colonial occupier. A fairy-tale, indeed. Translating Yi Sang involves unraveling and respinning his syllabic silks. Translators can and should change socks seasonally. We can even darn "browncoloredfurrysocks."

One of the stories that my father still remembers from his childhood is a tale about someone living utterly alone in such destitution that the walls of his room had no wallpaper—they were covered in newspaper instead. In Nagisa Oshima's

Death by Hanging (film, 1968)—a great work of satire that confronts Japan's imperial legacy and its discrimination against Zainichi Koreans—an execution chamber turns into a living room. (An incredible fairy-tale scene.) A Korean family is living in such abject poverty that their living-room walls are covered in newspaper. A while back, when I first attempted reading Yi Sang's poems, I sent my father photocopies of the poems from "Crow's Eye View" and asked him to decipher for me the Chinese characters Yi Sang utilized. My father sent back the photocopied pages with his meticulous notes, each character numbered and explained. For his daughter, he didn't try to cheat his way out of translation. I used the pages my father returned to me as wallpaper for Yi Sang's dark attic. Inside, there is a narrow staircase that takes you up to a tiny balcony, just big enough for a child or a bird.

䵂䵖會豕

　　그날밤에그의아내가층게에서굴러떨어지고—공연히내일일을글탄말라고 어느눈치빨은어룬이 타일러놓섰다. 옳고말고다. 그는하로치씩만잔뜩산(生)다. 이런복음에곱신히그는 덩어리(속지말라)처럼말(言)이없다. 잔뜩산다. 아내에게무엇을물어보리오? 그러니까아내는대답할일이생기지않고 따라서부부는식물처럼조용하다. 그러나식물은아니다. 아닐뿐아니라여간동물이아니다. 그래서그런지그는이굴궤짝만한방안에무슨연줄로언제부터이렇게있게되었는지도모지기억에없다. 오늘다음에오늘이있는것. 래일조금전에오늘이있는것. 이런것은영따지지않기로하고 그저 얼마든지 오늘 오늘 오늘 오늘 허릴없이눈가린마차말의동강난視야다. 눈을뜬다. 이번에는생시가보인다. 꿈에는생시를꿈꾸고생시에는꿈을꿈꾸고 어느것이나자미있다. 오후네시. 옴겨앉은아침—여기가아침이냐. 날마다. 그러나물론그는한번씩한번씩이다. (어떤巨大한母체가나를여기다갖다버렸나)—그저한없이게을른것—사람노릇을하는채대체어디얼마나기껏게을을수있나좀해보자—게을으자—그저한없이게을으자—시끄러워도그저몰은체하고게을으기만하면다된다. 살고게을르고죽고—가로대사는것이라면떡먹기다. 오후네시. 다른시간은다어디갔나. 대수냐. 하루가한시간도없는것이라기로서니무슨성화가생기나.

　　또 거미. 아내는꼭거미. 라고그는믿는다. 저것이어서도로환투를하여서거미형상을나타내었으면—그러나거미를총으로쏘아죽였다는이야기는들은일이없다. 보통 발로밟아죽이는데 신발신기커냥일어나기도싫다. 그러니까마찬가지다. 이방에 그외에또생각하야보면—맥이뼈를디디는것이빤이보이고, 요밖으로내어놓는팔뚝이밴댕이처럼꼬스르하다—이방이그냥거민게다. 그는거미속에가

넙적하게들어누어있는게다. 거미내음새다. 이후덥지근한내음새는 아하 거미
내음새다. 이방안이거미노릇을하느라고풍기는흉악한내음새에틀림없다. 그래
도그는아내가거미인것을잘알고있다. 가만둔다. 그리고기껏게을러서아내—
人거미—로하여금육체의자리—(或, 틈)를주지않게한다.

This excerpt shows the original spacing used in "Spider&SpiderMeetPigs"
when it first appeared in *Chungang*, June 1936.

SPIDER&SPIDERMEETPIGS

Thatnighthiswifefelldownthestairs—somequickwittedelderadvisedhim not-
toneedlessly worryabouttomorrow. Spoton. Helivestothefullestfullyonedayata-
time. Underthecommandofsuch gospelhegrovels silentlikeamute(Don'tbefooled).
Helivestothefullest. Askhiswifewhat? Hiswife doesn'treplybecausenothingever-
getssaid andthereforethecouplestaysquietlikeplants. Butthey aren'tplants. No-
tonlyaretheynotplantsbutnotevenanimals—atleastnotordinaryones. Maybe-
that's whyhecan'trememberatallhowheendedupwithhiswifeinaroomastinyasasa-
tsumaorangebox. Beyondtodaythere'sanothertoday. Justbeforetomorrowthere's
today. Whocaresexcept today today today today justlikethetunnelvisionofacoach-
horsewithblinderson. Opensheiseyes. Thistimereality appears. Inhisdreamhedreams
ofhisreallifeandinhisreallifehedreamsadream andthey'reboth amusing. Fourin-
theafternoon. Morninggotshifted—isitmorning? It'severyday. Butofcoursehe lives
fortodayonedayatatime. (Whatkindofhugepregnantthinghasdumpedmehere?)—
I'm perpetuallylazy—let'sseehowmuchmorelazyIcangetwhilepretendingtobehuman
—justwanttobe lazy—stayendlesslylazy—evenwhenthingsgetnoisyaroundmeall
Ihavetodoisstaytotallyoblivious andlazy. Livegetlazythendie—it'sapieceofcake.
Fourintheafternoon. Whathappenedtoallother hours? What'sthebigdeal? ThinkI'll
freakoutjustbecausethere'snotevenasinglehourinaday?

Spideragain. Mywifeisdefinitelyaspider hebelieves. Wishshewouldreincarnate
andreveal herspidershape—howeveroneneverhearsofanyonekillingaspiderwith
agunshot. Normally youstep onspidersandcrushthem butIcan'tbebotheredtoput
onmyshoesnevermindgettingup. It'sallthesame tome. Insidetheroom outsidethe-

roomwhenIthinkmoreaboutit—Icanseemyveinpulsingagainstmy skinnybone and mywristlaidontopoftheblanketisasscalyasaherring—thisroomissimplyas- pider. He'sstretchedoutinsideaspider. Spidersmell. Thiswarmstenchisthestench ofthespider. Theroomis givingoffanawfulstinkbecauseit'saspider. Howeverheknows verywellit'shiswifethat'sthespider. Heleavesheralone. Andheremainsaslazyashe canlyingaroundsohiswife—humanspider—willhave no(Notevenahintof)space.

Excerpted translation follows the original spacing.

SPIDER&SPIDERMEETPIGS[1]

1

That night his wife fell down the stairs—some quick-witted elder advised him not to needlessly worry about tomorrow.[2] Spot on. He lives to the fullest fully one day at a time. Under the command of such gospel, he grovels, silent like a mute (Don't be fooled). He lives to the fullest. Ask his wife what? His wife doesn't reply because nothing ever gets said, and therefore the couple stays quiet like plants. But they aren't plants. Not only are they not plants but not even animals—at least, not ordinary ones. Maybe that's why he can't remember at all how he ended up with his wife in a room as tiny as a satsuma orange box. Beyond today, there's another today. Just before tomorrow, there's today. Who cares except today today today today, just like the tunnel vision of a coach horse with blinders on. Opens his eyes. This time, reality appears. In his dream, he dreams of his real life and in his real life, he dreams a dream, and they're both amusing. Four in the afternoon. Morning got shifted—is it morning? It's every day. But of course, he lives for today, one day at a time. (What kind of huge, pregnant thing has dumped me here?)—I'm perpetually lazy—let's see how much more lazy I can get while pretending to be human—just want to be lazy—stay endlessly lazy—even when things get noisy around me, all I have to do is stay totally oblivious and lazy. Live, get lazy, then die—it's a piece of cake. Four in the afternoon. What happened to all other hours? What's the big deal? Think I'll freak out just because there's not even a single hour in a day?

Spider again. My wife is definitely a spider, he believes. Wish she would reincarnate and reveal her spider shape—however one never hears of anyone killing a spider with a gunshot. Normally, you step on spiders and crush them, but I can't be bothered to put on my shoes, never mind getting up. It's all the same to me. Inside the room, outside the room, when I think more about it—I can see my vein pulsing against my skinny bone, and my wrist laid on top of the blanket is as scaly as a herring—this room is simply a spider. He's stretched out inside a spider. Spider smell. This warm stench is the stench of the spider. The room is giving off an awful stink because it's a spider. However, he knows very well it's his wife that's the spider. He leaves her alone. And he remains as lazy as he can, lying around so his wife—human spider—will have no (Not even a hint of) space.

Outside the room, his wife's shuffling around. She's making breakfast, too early for tomorrow's morning and too late for today's. He briskly closes the door. (Quickly) A cabinet covered in multicolored paper goes out of sight. It's hideous. He despises household goods altogether. What's he supposed to do with them anyway? Why does today exist? So that he has to stare at the cabinet? It's getting dark. He stays lazy so that today and the cabinet will vanish. But his wife is startled. He closes the door—husband—her husband who is supposed to be asleep, so she begins to wonder. Maybe he needs to take a leak—perhaps he's itchy—why did he wake up? What's astonishing to her is that—how does he live the way he does?— and what's even more astonishing is how he sleeps. How does he keep on sleeping like that? Everything about them was abnormal. Husband. What makes them a married couple?—husband—even if she weren't his wife, she's ultimately a wife. But she thinks, what has my husband ever done for me?—he's never even shielded me from a cold draft. As if frightened—she certainly is—she opens the door and speaks to her husband with that voice of hers, unfamiliar no matter how many times you hear it. Sweetheart—today's *Christmas*—it's warm like a spring day (Not the source of their ruin), so please shave.

His wife's cumbersome spider legs refuse to vanish from his head, yet what she's said about *Christmas* feels ice cold. How did they end up as husband and wife? It's true that his wife is the one who pursued him, but why did she pursue him? No. Why didn't she leave him?—that's certain. When it became certain that she wasn't going to leave him—after they were stuck as a couple for a year and a half—she left him. He was clueless as to why his wife had left him. That's why he had no idea how to find her. But his wife returned. And he knew why. Now, he knows why his wife's not leaving him. That surely portends his wife is about to leave him again. At least that's how things seem, based on his experience. But then he can't keep pretending not to know. He simply hopes that if his wife ends up leaving him again, she'll come right back to him—even if he'll know all along why she won't come back.

He shaved then went out to the street where everything had closed. As has been noted, *Christmas* was as warm as a spring day. The sun must have grown bigger while he's been away. The sun was too bright for his eyes—his skin coarse, dry— his legs heavy, and he got out of breath just staring at wall after wall stuck to the buildings. His wife's white socks changed into brown-colored furry socks— weather had only existed as a news item while he was hiding out in his room. Winter—that arrived even before the end of autumn, he gave out a cough as if he were greeting it for the very first time. A winter's day warm like a spring day—perhaps a holiday like this was common all over the world—but the wind felt cold against his cheeks and nostrils. The bustling crowd, the shoeshine boy carrying a heavy box, yelling, and all the shut windows were unbearably suffocating to him. He gasped. Where to now? (A Investments) (Remembers a business card) (Mr. O) (Stop boasting) (The 24 is payday) As if conversing with someone he gestured with his arms and circled around the paper-thin walls of A Investments, wondering what's inside. Air? Fierce air. Freezing air—no ordinary air. O's bloodshot eyes— red-hot telephone—his disheveled body looking as if it might combust. O's name was inscribed on the chair as on a bottle cap. It was like a dream. Handsome O was having a jolly, jolly life, going through the ledger, recording addresses and names one by one. He had the whole office to himself, with a sign, "Research Division," at the door, and he had covered all four walls with paintings on graph paper, none of which were really art.

Spider: "If you analyze those things long enough, you'll be able to guess more or less."

O: "Tally up, then money doesn't seem like money."

Spider: "If not money, graph paper?"

O: "Graph paper?"

Spider: "Yes, and what about the total sum?"

O: "Hmm—I feel like painting again."

However, it was difficult for O to endure his work without it destroying him. If not alcohol—art? O let everything hang out. Likewise, he (Spider) shuts down in front of O and the world. Why? Because I'm a spider. I'm getting as thin as a pencil—no blood flows through my veins—mind's still there even when it's not thinking—a clogged mind—useless ideas—never exit the spider, spider—never look out —drunk—confused—the room—room looks like a traditional pointed sock. His wife. Because she's a spider.

O stopped jotting down addresses and names and offered him a cigarette. Then the door opened, cutting through the smoke. (At closing hour) Some fat man dashed in like a horse. The fatty gentleman greeted O. Slim O with a deep voice and the fatty gentleman with a soft voice chatted away.

Fatty: "Is the director out?"

O: "Yes—ah, we are just over two hundred clients."

Fatty: "That's plenty. He may arrive earlier."

O: "I'll get there an hour early."

Fatty: "Yes—and yes—and yesand yesand, I see."

O: "You're going now?"

After the brisk exchange, the fatty gentleman threw him (Spider) a glance, turned his head as if he were about to leave, then threw another glance at him. He (Spider)—I wonder what would happen if I said hello? He hesitated then on impulse bowed to the fatty gentleman. How inappropriate. The fatty gentleman accepted his bow, then left, grinning. What an insult. Even while he was trying to remember who the fatty gentleman was, his mocking reply, "How are things?" was ringing in his ears. What did he mean by How are things?—now who is he?—right, right. The fatty gentleman was the owner of *Café* R at the banquet hall, where his wife worked. His wife had returned to him three months ago. She said she'd returned to keep him fed and alive. When he got the loan (One hundred *won*[3]) he stood his wife before Fatty and closed the deal with his oval-shaped seal. Just because today is today, he couldn't have possibly forgotten the humiliation he felt when he saw Fatty dressed in a *yukata*,[4] looking down his nose at him. But before he recognized Fatty, he'd unknowingly bowed his head to him. Now. Now. The memory of Fatty must have seeped into the marrow of his bones. With his dark, obsessive disposition—it doesn't make sense that he would bow to him unknowingly. Disgusting. What's my excuse? Shit! Shit—fine, I won't blame myself—I promise. Yet his cheeks were burning up. And his eyes got teary. Spider—I'm a spider for sure. Know that you are sucking the life out of your wife who's getting skinny like a cigarette holder. I'm spider. My mouth reeks. And my wife, doesn't she also suck me dry? Take a look—my bruised, shaved chin—my sunken eyes—my skinny, near-malnourished body. My wife's a spider. She couldn't be anything else. Spider and spider, spider and spider? Sucking on each other? Where are they headed? Why are they becoming so scrawny? One morning a bone poked through her skin—his wife's palm-sized forehead perspired. He placed his hand on her forehead, then callously stepped on her. Around midnight, his wife let out a squeal like a mouse, crinkled. Then opened up like a drawstring pouch the next morning. She bloomed like a castor bean, a garish flower. Their room flooded every night and rubbish piled up in a matter of two days[5]—his wife took a big load of garbage out late morning—four in the afternoon—he returned after dumping the garbage out in the field for her. His wife was becoming thin as a rail. The flower was sadistic like metal—sadistic spider—shut the door. He'd put a cap on life, stopped all habitual human relations, and he'd shut down. From all friends—from all relations—from all hopes—from all greed—from all profanities—he could only get hysterical in his room. He licked whatever he wanted as he would seaweed. The light bulb easily burnt out from his panting. Every night the room got weary, caused a ruckus, and gradually got ill, but the room toughed it out. Room swooned.[6] The world outside—no matter how long it waited for him, he didn't go out. He only watched life march by through a small glass window, palm sized. But night quickly shut down even such a tiny hole. No.

O lowered the window *shutters* as if he couldn't bear to see him (Spider) looking embarrassed. Let's go out. But he (Spider) wanted to return to his room without leaving the office. (6 *won* rental) (Nothing else but a room) (A comfy room) I only wish.

O: "How do you know Fatty?"

Spider: "I just do."

O: "What do you mean 'just'?"

Spider: "I just do."

O: "Are you two close?"

Spider: "Certainly not—so what does he do?"

O: "He—he's a gambler—he's invested ten thousand *won* through our firm."

Spider: "Hmm."

O: "The country bumpkin wants to be a hotshot."

Spider: "Hmm."

Café R appeared to be Fatty's side gig. Tomorrow night, A Investments would hold a year-end party for their clients on the third floor of *Café* R, and O was in charge of the preparations. So later, O stopped by the banquet hall at *Café* R. First, they had tea. Music flowed out from a turntable next to the *Christmas tree*. His fur coat long like a traditional outer-robe—his oiled hair—his gold watch—his jewel-studded tiepin—O's entire garb irritated him to no end. How did he get so sleazy? No, how did I end up like this? (Money) O was a con artist. He cleaned everyone out then chased them off with no more than bus fare to their names. Thirty thousand to a million *won*. Women couldn't keep their hands off him. O advised (Spider) to make the most of his youth like him, and not aimlessly loiter about. (O's smooth talk) How?—I have no clue how I've fallen so far behind O. Yet O's crude boasting sounded like a pure lie, so he couldn't bring himself to feel envious even if he was, as there was something that didn't make sense about it all.

Last spring, O was in Incheon. Ten years—their innocent friendship, their dreams, their days of youth were a beautiful memory. In early spring, with nothing yet in bloom, (Spider) in poor health walked with O along a mountain trail and listened to what O urgently had to say. Unexpectedly—O's father had lost his entire fortune of a million *won*, and the final auction had ended the day before—O pulled from his pocket a desperate note from his elderly father, a rice speculator who'd placed his last strand of hope on O out of several of his children—O couldn't betray his father—O wept—his father begged O to give up his dream of becoming an artist in this time of crisis, a mutual dream of O's and his (Spider's)—it was the first and the last confession O had spilt. At the time, he (Spider) was just waiting for his health to improve and spring to arrive—he had also secretly given up on painting a while back—he only stared at the wet paint that will soon dry and crack. Then a cyclone came. Come—come see my life—he laughed at O's summons and went to visit him in Incheon. FourFour—bustling waterfront—the office of K Invest-ments—his ill health still showing in his eyes, he watched in disbelief O's impec-cable professional conduct and lamented the new day, new day about to arrive. Ex-cept for where the phone was, every space was filled with graph paper. The cheap, cracked sheets were painted up and down with red and blue lines—O's face changed every minute of the day. At night he followed O and went barhopping till late—(*Shikishima Bar*)—his (Spider) body was getting thinner by the day, but strangely enough, O could get right back up at six in the morning, roll around his bloodshot eyes, his red cheeks looking fine as ever, and never fail to show up at his waterfront office by nine o'clock. O's tireless body together with his boundless energy—inevitably—appeared to be channeling some kind of force. In the after-noons, O's depressed father played a *kayagŭm*,[7] all that remained of his fortune, and happily jotted things down in his small notebook whenever he received a call from his only trustworthy son. Through the open sliding door, he could sometimes spot the Seoul–Incheon train. He put on O's fur coat and strolled around Wŏlmi Is-land and lay down flat on his back on the grass between the two trees not fully in bloom, dismayed that his ill health still persisted even though spring had arrived. The view of the sea—waves crashed onto the muddy shores and the day grew darker and darker. Every day, at four in the afternoon, O, whistling, came to find him on the same grassy spot. Under the tarp, they listened to the swaying *portable* radio, drank tea, watched a deer go by, then had *ice cream* on the long sea bank, watching the clam diggers, and ended the evening jovially together reading a news-paper at O's place. A month went by like this—May—he learned to sing a folk song, "Follow the Boat," on the same grassy spot. The big plans deeply seeded in his heart dissipated out to the sea one by one. When he returned from Incheon to his room, carrying with him endless doubts about life, his wife was nowhere to be found. At last, his wife's letting him know what he is really, a rebellious kid—(Literature)

(Poetry)—who walks a lost road to push life away, but when he wants to escape again—defiant youth (Politics)—he phones the *tourist bureau*. It was only in his room that the ship heading out to the ocean blew its horn and returned to port. While he was sweating, the summer passed—but before the sweat dried up on his back, his wife returned anxiously, looking like a tattered postcard stamped "Return to Sender." She said she wanted to support him, a starving artist, buried in old journals. The returned postcard—half of which was missing—he closed his eyes and smelled the distinct scent of her flesh. He'd needlessly put effort into the story of his everyday life. It has ended. Feed me, I'll eat—get a haircut—a cheap perm iron—he could lounge around all day in his underwear—*Café* R—a hundred *won* he borrowed from Fatty in a *yukata*—then he ran to O with the money in his hand, for O's plot was ringing in his ears—bring me a hundred *won*, I'll put down a hundred, and within three months I'll give you back five hundred—O sounded totally convincing. Out of her own guilt, his wife kept quiet even though she knew he had taken the money. He was conned. He stared at the boat schedule in the paper. O wrote a few times and highly praised his (Spider) life. O came to Seoul. It had been three months last month—he told me to dump my wife (Even though he didn't refer to her as my wife) despite the fact that she was the one who was supplying O in Incheon with every bit she earned—oh, that deal, O's priceless, deep friendship had clearly erased any memory about the five hundred *won* he was supposed to hand over last month—a few days ago O's delightful letter burrowed into his closed-off life. He slept through fall and winter. He was in the middle of his sleep when the letter arrived—hey buddy, how could you take in the ruined girl and live with her again?—O's useless attempt at stirring things up irritated him—and it wasn't—*Christmas*. Let me take a good look at O's guilt-free face—his splendid face—O of the past—that's it—I'll draw a circle around today's date before things really get out of control—and of course his wife didn't know a thing.

2

That night his wife fell down the stairs. It was unsightly.

He had a drink with O, whom he could no longer read or even recognize. They didn't drink at the *café* his wife worked at, but then he couldn't find any other place that differed even the slightest bit from *Café* R and was horrified to see so many of his wives. What an insane world. All these places were set up exactly the same, so it was hard to tell one from another—O says—you can tell by which girls are going into which *cafés*—at two in the afternoon men poured into them, and he (Spider) had already heard about the intriguing lives of the barmaids who received the men one at a time, those who played their husbands. His wife reminded him of the duty toward her, and she had reproached him several times for not coming out to greet her after work, but he worried about being seen—but by whom?—which is to say— the ugly, flat-faced world. He looked around the indistinguishable, makeup-crusted faces—the only way you could tell them apart was whether they had on high- or low-quality makeup. I'm sure all men say this—in the private room of the *café*—hee hee—(You look just like my wife)—but my wife hardly used any makeup —my wife's light freckles—her itty-bitty nose—her lips thinner than any thin lips —(What if your made-up face looks like my wife's with no makeup?)—"forgive me"—but why is my wife so frail? What's making her so thin? (Your fault) (You really don't know?) (I know) but take a look at this woman. She's as plump as well-risen dough. O whispered into my ears, It gets unbearably hot when she sits right next to you.

"This Miss Fatty is Mayumi—she's a Yankee pig,[8] but she's marvelous, marvel-ous—you know (I know) the story of the goose that laid the golden eggs? She's a pot of gold—in just one night she makes three *won*, four *won*, five *won*—she's like a pawnshop that lends out money for nothing. (Really?) Oh—she's my beloved Ma-yumi."

By now my wife must be doing the same thing as Mayumi. This hurts. O immediately chuckled at his (Spider) frowning face. Ha—it's foul—but listen—a rice speculator's girl is totally taboo. But what am I s'posed to do, when she's shoving her flesh into my mouth? (Right, right) What's a girl anyway? Girls are nothing without money—no, money without girls is meaningless. (Right, right) Come on, keep going. When I catch one, I buy a gold watch, several in fact, gemstones, and fur coats, all expensive. When I lose one, I seduce again, right? (Right, right) But this is a bit pathetic. But what I do is pick a bitchy girl and buy her a watch, jewelry, then take them back from her, then seduce her again, buy things again, take them back again, then seduce her—I really do buy them for the girl, but they are ultimately mine—after a while—I can only use girls, by the way—she hands over whatever she has earned in one night—I mean she's shoving her flesh into my mouth, so at least she can hand over three, four *won*—I keep buying her jewelry, so even if she has nothing left, it's only fair, so I'm bloodsucking spider, I know I'm pimping spider—no, it's not like I don't fulfill her demands—but it gets to be a nuisance when she demands we rent a room and live together—hey, if I go that far then my dream of making a million by the time I'm thirty will go bust. (Right? Right?) Those who become beggars now outnumber those who become rich later, wishing for a cow, so to be safe you need to have a girl like that. You're basically fighting with your back to the sea. And O's cunning, so he'll never in a million years divvy up the boat with the goose that lays the golden eggs. Those cheeks caked with makeup, those thick lips, nothing could be more adorable to him.

His (Spider) eyes looked wasted and he entered, tipsy, from drinking. His glassy eyes observed Mayumi the lump of meat as if in envy. Wife—Mayumi—wife—my wife who keeps getting skinny—my skewer-thin wife—stop getting so thin—take a look at Mayumi—her ample bust and chubby face, puff, puff, puff—life's not fair— one puffs up like a corn cracker and the other shrinks, barely visible—let's see—

he could see her body bloating up like a toasted rice cake. But his eyeballs only wiggled up and down like the goldfish inside a fish tank. He could only faintly see Mayumi's pudgy face moving slowly like seaweed. O giggled, screamed, clapped, and giggled again inside the stink of her makeup.

Why is it that only O has this power? O has definitely prevented Mayumi from becoming thin. He probably ordered her to stay fat. Impressive. Power. Will—? Such power—where does it come from? Yes—if I had it I wouldn't be wasted—I would work—excel at it—I want to throw myself out the window. I want to untie and throw down my wife's obstinate apron strings and freely run away. I want all the things that my will has not acted on to disappear. I'll shut down. Layer by layer. But then what could this be if not power?—his ferocious, bloodshot eyes, searching for a breathing hole on the flickering wall of ecstasy. He trembled. He had merely turned into a pathetic drunk, unable to tell apart before and after, as if a tornado had struck inside an empty skull.

At that moment, Mayumi whispered into his ear. He shrugged his neck as he stuck out his tongue, wag, wagging it. Anyway, I think I ate too much—I'm also drunk too, but I am too full. Mayumi, what are you trying to say?

"Do you think I don't know that O is a liar? I know (That's what) makes him an artist. He'll do something entirely different than he says. Please tell him—not to deceive me—that Mayumi is not going to be fooled—I'm pleading with you because I've fallen for him somewhat—you know, mister? (Of course I know) Whatever, I can't live without this shitty lifeline. (What? What?) Think about it—what's the point of making three, four *won* every night?—to buy makeup? Clothes? But then I buy the most expensive stuff once or twice, actually a dozen times—but I can't keep buying all that stuff every single day. What would I do with it all?—after a while I get tired of it—then do I give it away to beggars?—nothing more despicable in this world than to have your things repossessed. But it's much better to have a lifeline than makeup and clothes. I never get tired of him—a cheater—no—it's a bit different. We fight, then I lose what I earn to my lifeline that same night—no, I feel so good after I hand over everything I have to him. Sweet. So basically, I'm raising a spider to suck on me with my own hands. But then my lifeline simply fills the void in me, so I don't feel bad about losing everything; instead I wonder if he's a spider indeed. This can all end if I don't make any money, but this lifestyle is smeared into my flesh, so it's not easy to end it right way, and I don't want it to end. He grits his teeth and steals from me."

Socks—he (Spider) thought about his wife's socks. Strangely, notes and silver coins fell out from her socks every night. When the fifty *jŏn*[9] dropped onto the floor and made a jingling sound, it was certainly the most incomparably sublime sound in the world. I wonder how many of those silver coins her shins will spit out—her legs that looked like dried pollock had coin marks on them—money bored into her flesh—sucking on every bit of her strength. Oh—spider—the forgotten spider—money is also spider—but in front of my eyes, robust twin spiders—unbelievably robust, aren't they? He lights a cigarette—really—Wife. What do you think I am that you're willing to keep me alive by doing this shitty work?—dying—living—I'm nobody. His existence was too hilarious. He mocked himself severely.

However—two o'clock—he walked quickly toward—his glamorous cave—room. After passing several alleys—O, you go wherever—every time I look at the bright warm window, window—hen—dog—cow, just like in a story—and the postcard— I clutch onto my boiling heart and dive into my steaming-hot room. All of my blood—weight—they must be here already—waiting for me—haven't been this drunk in a long while—as if my spine has dissolved, you bastard—you bastard— slurring ridiculously—I'll take a deep breath. Breathe harder. And endure. Shit. Just lose it.

But what's going on? Wife was waiting in the room. Ah-ha—that day has arrived.

That day when you leave and I don't have a clue why—why today of all days? And (Before I knew why you returned) while I go on not knowing why you've left, you've come back again—so pointless. Should I just shut down altogether? That way, even if I fall into a sewer, the world can't mock me, even if it wants to—don't give her any reason to nitpick me. *Café* R—tomorrow A Investments is hosting its year-end client party—my wife—the bow Fatty accepted from me—looking disheveled, he slowly walked through the back door and up to the *cho-ba*[10] counter of the damn *Café* R. *Cho-ba*? I know all about it—I know how much you buy things for, then sell at what price—what's the point of knowing—hey you, lady with glasses on, let me ask you a question. (It's bustling in here. How do they all live inside here?) One by one, the lady stamped paper slips that looked like report cards. My wife always said this. Regardless of how much you earn, you must pay back only a *won*—or no interest paid—why no interest?—(Do you know?)—money—doesn't seem like money?—did you total up? Yes.

"Where is Namiko?"

"Are you her husband? She's at the police station."

"What did she do wrong?"

The *cook* came out, holding a knife in his hand, as if to say—what are you, an idiot? Listen up. Your wife fell down the stairs—why are you so skinny?—ouch, ouch, let me go, let me explain, ouch, ouch, let me go. (With teary eyes) Why are you so fat like a Yankee pig?—what? a Yankee pig?—if not a Yankee pig then what?— you bitch.

That is why Namiko got kicked and rolled, rolled down the stairs, it's outrageous—all too outrageous.

"She wasn't hurt badly, but she needed to learn a lesson, so I called the police."

How dare she talk back to the gracious customer who jokingly called her a bag of bones, she was out of line calling him a Yankee pig—think about it, if you're not a bag of bones then what are you?—right—if I were called a Yankee pig—no, called a bag of bones—no, called a Yankee pig—no, no, called a bag of bones—in fact, I'm also a bag of bones—no, I couldn't have put up with it—I would have no choice but to call him a Yankee pig—but no, how could she call me a Yankee pig, and if I were a customer—no, if I were a barmaid—nonsense—if I were a customer, I would have beaten the shit out of you. But, Wife, you did well by calling him a Yankee pig, and that's why he kicked you—why, whose side am I taking? I'm sure her rickety, rickety body got hurt—like broken plates—this hurts. Hurts. Before I lost hope, a *saburo*[11] came over, panting. He asked for Namiko's husband to follow him. I'm the one—a good chance to get my word in. He's a son of a bitch. Please charge him. The barmaids and busboys and kitchen *itabas*[12] were so firmly on Namiko's side that the whole situation felt even more outlandish.

The jail cell—how odd—the assistant inspector and the police officer and O and Fatty the owner of *Café* R and the Yankee Pig–like culprit (Yankee Pig would have slipped out of my mouth too) and his wife, crunched up in front of the heater, terrified like a mouse—he looked up and down at this most unlikely *combination* of characters in amazement. He staggered up to Yankee Pig and stared long at his greasy face then, "Are you the one? Are you the one?"

Pig remained nonchalant. Pig and Spider stared at each other while grinning inside—but Wife, wait a minute—please stop crying, let me try talking to him. Huff. As he let out a deep breath—the nausea he'd been holding at bay surged up all at once till he felt like he was going to pass out. With his shirttail hanging out of his pants, he spoke to Yankee Pig.

Pig: "You look pretty weak."

Spider: "You're changing the topic."

Pig: "What do you mean?"

Spider: "You're changing the topic."

Pig: "What do you mean I'm changing the topic?"

Spider: "Ha, you're changing the topic!"

Pig: "Ha, what do you mean I'm changing the topic?"

The inspector yelled, unable to stand anymore of this. Are you Namiko's husband? Your name? Your occupation? He could only sheepishly bow his head lower at each question. Don't just bob your head up and down, are you going to make a charge against him? What do you want to do? Yes, I want to. (In your eyes, I'm not even a maggot. So if I don't know what to do, shouldn't you police officers know? And are you saying that you'll really do as I say?) Who should you really be asking? O, who's standing over there, and my wife's pimp should tell me what to do. Tears were already streaming down his cheeks. He felt more and more intoxicated. He wasn't in his right mind and had no courage to open his mouth. O and Fatty tapped his shoulder to comfort him.

"He's A Investments's executive director. He was just drunk. As you already know, tomorrow is our year-end party, so if we don't have our director there, then it would be as bad as not having our president there. Is there any way you can reconcile?"

Spider: "Reconcile for whose sake?"

O: "For your friend's."

Spider: "What friend?"

O: "Then for our firm's."

Spider: "Are you the boss?"

Fatty interjected,

"Then for your wife's."

I had borrowed from Fatty a hundred *won* twice. I still owe him a hundred fifty *won*—I get it. He's threatening me.

"This is going to sound like a fairy tale, but this actually happened. It's an amazing story about a hundred *won* that's supposed to become five hundred *won* in just three months, yet by the fourth month all the money vanished without a trace. (O, am I embarrassing you?) So what does it matter that a mere barmaid got kicked? (O, it's okay, okay) I'm going. Why are you all kicking up a fuss? I want to mind my own business. Let me sober up quietly. Please let me go. I'll take my wife with me. Then you can all do whatever you want."

Night—the first night the flood dried up—incredibly dry night. Wife, you can't get any thinner than you already are. Definitely not. That's an order. Wife was ill, frail like a sparrow, whimpering from fever all night long. Shamelessly, he fell deeply asleep as soon as he crashed beside her. He even snored, though he usually never snored—oh—who's really the Yankee pig? He was exhausted. He was simply dumbfounded.

Meanwhile—long hours.

Wife went out in the morning. Because that *saburo* came for her. He asked her to go to the police station. He (Spider) was asked to come along as well. But he didn't want to budge one bit. He sent his wife instead even though she was limping, then let out a big sigh—humanity, ugh. Best to be endlessly lazy. He closed all the doors in a row, now alone without his wife's whimpering—hope things take a while so she won't return till later in the evening—he even wished his wife would leave him altogether. He longed to fall asleep with his legs stretched out.

Two o'clock in the afternoon—two bills of ten *won*. His wife couldn't stop grinning ear to ear in front of him.

"Who gave them to you?"

"Your friend O."

O, O, so it was O. (He's the protagonist of my fairy tale who gulped down my hundred *won*) My memories of the lost youth I long for are changing. Everything is changing. Even if I shut myself inside my room, not shaving, lounging around for an entire year, twelve months, the world seeps in through the walls, and with it that cruel stench of humanity, ugh. He hasn't slept this long in a while. His mind was getting clearer, clearer.

Spider: "O gave them to you? What did he say when he gave them to you?"

Spider: "That the director is very sorry and that he apologized as soon as he got sober."

Spider: "So where did you end up going?"

Spider: "To the *cho-ba*."

Spider: "Good going. So you just accepted the money?"

Spider: "I wasn't going to, but O said that the director was truly sorry."

So it wasn't O's money. Was it the director's then? It's possible that the two Fatties colluded. Did they each cover half, ten *won* each? Why's his mind so clear at a time like this? He wished he were so groggy that he couldn't think at all. The year-end party in the afternoon. The charge. The compensation. The maggot. Wife's no better than a maggot. She kept whining about her aches and pains.

"Since we got free money, let's spend it. I won't go to work today. (She doesn't think of buying an ointment for her bruises, not even in her dreams) Tomorrow afternoon, I can get a roll of fabric for my skirt, another for my blouse (One of what? One of what?) (After she blows ten *won*), then with the remaining ten, I'll have a pair of shoes custom-made for you."

Do whatever you want. I'm sleepy. Unbearably sleepy. Don't bother me even if I sniffle. Right now, on the third floor of *Café* R an important banquet is taking place and Fatty Director will be looking very proper with his shirt all tucked in. From jail to banquet (From factory to home) a piddling twenty *won*—two hundred clients—turkey—ham—sausages—lard—a Yankee pig—one-year-old, two-year-old, ten-year-old—beard—like cold ash—all that's left are—bones—messy stains —what else is left?—all through his yearlong shutdown mode—January's mouth gaped in front of him, while he was rotting away, still alive.

She must have felt comforted by him, nevertheless. She fell deeply asleep. The light bulb gazed down at them as if pitying them. These two didn't drink water all day long. Because of twenty *won* the couple was able to totally violate the solemn law—one must eat in order to stay alive.

This most repulsive biological organism felt hunger. I'm hungry. How pathetic. How embarrassing. But, O, if you compare your life to mine, no, my life to yours, whose is truly superior? No, whose is truly inferior? He put on his coat and hat— didn't forget to put twenty *won* in his pocket—left his room. Night was fogged in. The air was foul as if it were rotting. Again—spider, of course. (Money exchange)— he put his finger under his nose and sniffed it. Spider smell—but it smelled more like the vinegary smell of the twenty *won* bill he rubbed between his fingers. This sour smell—because of it the whole world has to sometimes corrupt the innocent —not only sometimes! How much it sickens everyone. He couldn't control his con- flicting emotions. Spider—right—I'm the one and only spider. Watch me. Watch where my sticky tentacles point next—he broke out in goose bumps and a cold sweat.

Angry tentacles—Mayumi—O's assertive girl—lifelines—loneliness—there's no way around it. The twenty *won* in his hand—Mayumi—spend ten *won* on drinks and ten on tips, and if Mayumi still refuses me, I'll call her Yankee Pig. If that still doesn't do the trick, then twenty *won*'s blown—wasted—so what? It's free. The di- rector can kick my wife down the stairs again. Then I'll have twenty *won* again. Ten *won* on drinks, ten on tips. And if Mayumi still refuses, then I'll call her Yankee Pig. If that doesn't do it, then twenty *won* is blown. Wife, please whisper into the direc- tor's ear again and call him Yankee Pig. And if he kicks you, just shut up and roll down the stairs.

June 1936

1. In the original text, Yi Sang utilizes Chinese characters to create a new word for the title: 鼅鼄會豕. The first two characters both mean "spider," so he is referring to two spiders in the story: "he" and "Wife"—the husband and wife spiders. The third character means "to meet." The fourth refers to pigs. Hence "Spider&SpiderMeetPigs." Yi Sang also experiments with the Korean language by disregarding any conventional breaks between words and phrases. The excerpts closely follow the original text, published in *Chungang* (1936). This second version follows the standardized version in Korean with conventional breaks.

2. "not to needlessly worry about tomorrow": this phrase is believed to be in reference to Matthew 6:34. As cited in *Yi Sang Chŏnjip* (2013), compiled by Kwon Youngmin.

3. *won*: a Korean currency

4. *yukata*: a Japanese word for a light gown worn in summer.

5. The spiders' room behaves in some ways like a body with its own circadian rhythms, producing garbage as a kind of bodily waste; comparably surreal, bodily rooms may be found in the work of the contemporary Korean master-poet Kim Hyesoon. See her poem "The Road to Kimp'o Landfill":

THE ROAD TO KIMP'O LANDFILL

Cut my hair short again
I don't want to pull out
the names etched onto my hair that grows daily
As rain fell, garbage bins from the 2nd, 3rd, 4th floor
must have been turned upside down
Hair fell profusely
I kissed in a place where garbage came down like rain
I kissed where I vomited all night long
Every time I sang, vomit flew in
I turned the garbage bins upside down in my room
and had morning sickness, then had a smoke
My poetry books burned
Three hundred million babies were born
One hundred million of the young and the old died
The day I took the pills
I walked out the gate in the middle of my bath
Black plastic bags flew higher than a flock of sparrows
The discarded sewing machine was like the head of
    a horse
The sound of Mother's sewing machine
filled the holes in my body one by one
I tore off my swollen breasts and tossed them
beneath Mother's foot on the pedal
A forest gave off a foul smell, carried contagious
    diseases
It burned of fever during the night
A busboy at brightly lit Motel Rose
threw out millions of sperm every night
From the forest, mosquitoes swarmed
and dug into my scrawny caved-in chest
Born in the 20th century, I was on my way
to die in the 21st century

(From *Mommy Must Be a Fountain of Feathers* [2008], translated by Don Mee Choi.)

6. For another glimpse of the connection between Yi Sang's work and the grotesquely embodied rooms of Kim Hyesoon, consider her poem "Seoul's Dinner." In this poem, the entire city is internalized as a room, as a body:

SEOUL'S DINNER

Flowers enter. The flowers with puckered lips. The flowers that fill the back of a truck suck on the wall of the tunnel. The tunnel ripens red momentarily. She plucks off the new leaves and shoves them into her mouth. Angelica shoots drop from angelica trees and fall into the dish of seasoned soy sauce. A truckload of angelica enters. Angelica shoots turn the mouth of Seoul green. Flatfish enter. A thousand flatfish packed in ice enter, swooning. A truckload of the East Sea enters. Pigs enter. The pigs oink and suck on Seoul's lips. She dips the meat from the pig's neck in pickled shrimp and eats. Her squirming throat is omnivorous. Mudfish pour in like a muddy stream. The T'aebaek range is shredded and enters, squirming. The alpine fields of Mount Sŏrak enter, salted. Radishes revealing only the top half of their white bottoms are neatly stacked onto a truck. Trucks with their lights on enter. They line up and enter in between the teeth. When the trucks leave the tunnel, Seoul's dark-blue stomach acid covers them. Some of the trucks with big eyes try to make their way through the sea of acid, but the darkness inside Seoul's intestines is dense. Vegetables in sacks enter. Thousands of chickens with reddened crowns follow thousands of eggs just laid today and enter. Bulls as big as elephants, their eyes fiercely opened, enter. Bulls charge the road inside of someone who lives in Seoul. Tonight she drinks too much soju. The tunnel where the liquor is poured is long and dark. White milk that could overflow Lake Soyang pours out of the tunnel into the night's intestines. The plains of Honam enter. But in the opposite lane, trucks loaded with septic tanks have lined up in single file. Having left the party, I begin to vomit as soon as I step outside. Seoul eats and shits through the same door. My body curls up like a worm. It seems that every few days a big hand descends from the sky to roll out cloud-like toilet paper and wipe the opening of Seoul, which is simultaneously a mouth and an anus. Tonight, fat flakes fall as the last truck leaves the tunnel. I let the snow collect, then shove it into my mouth.

(From *Poor Love Machine* [2016], translated by Don Mee Choi.)

7. *kayagŭm*: a Korean twelve-stringed instrument

8. Yankee pig: *yangdweji*—"*yang*" in Korean means "Western," so the literal meaning is "Western pig." We chose Yankee instead of Western for the translingual pun, but also because the United States was the first Western nation to forge a treaty with Korea, in 1882, six years after Korea had signed a treaty with Japan.

In Yi Sang's world of colonial domination, even a helpless victim such as the spider husband who is taken advantage of by colonial capitalist collaborators is ultimately a Yankee pig in his relationship with his spider wife. As a woman in a highly patriarchal society, she is stepped on by everyone—both the colonizer and the colonized. In this spider-eat-spider, pig-eat-pig world, a willing victim, Mayumi, a.k.a. Miss Fatty, kept fattened by her pimp, is well mirrored in Kim Hyesoon's epic poem, "I'm OK, I'm Pig!" written in the current context of neocolonial domination. This poem is based on the fate of over a million pigs that were buried alive due to an outbreak of foot-and-mouth disease, a few years after the free-trade agreement between South Korea and the US was concluded in 2007. Excerpts from "I'm OK, I'm Pig!":

Pig9   Please raise and eat me
Pig9   Please cry after eating me
Pig9   I'll give birth to piglets
Pig9   Please say for once that you had a sad life
Pig9   Please wrap me up well and prepare me for a
        meal
Pig9   Please hang my intestines on a string
Pig9   Please don't throw away any part of me
Pig9   Please don't burp so loudly

—

Filthy filthy filthy I'm so filthy
I should just live in my dream, why did I come here?

Die, Pig!
Why do you suck on milk?
Why do you grow up?
I wouldn't if I were you
Master comes and feels how thick your fingers have
        become
How your flesh has plumped up
I wouldn't grow up if I were you
Oh there goes beloved Pig
It's chased out

—

Waking pill
Sleeping pill
Outing pill
Vomiting pill
Pill induced pill vomiting pill

—

(From *Sorrowtoothpaste Mirrorclean* [2014], translated by Don Mee Choi.)

Yi Sang's drawings of pills: Aspirin and sedatives—Adalin and Allonal "Roche"—for his short story "Wings," which first appeared in the magazine *Chogwang* (1936).

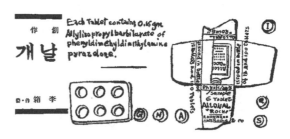

Note the letters of Yi Sang's name on each pill: RI SANG.

9. *jŏn*: a Korean coin

10. *cho-ba*: a Japanese word for "cash counter"

11. *saburo*: a Japanese word for "low-ranking police officer"

12. *itaba*: a Japanese word for "cook"

TRUE STORY—LOST FLOWER[1]

1

Having—

no secret is like having no wealth at all, poor and lonely. . .[2]

2

Dream—wish this was all a dream. But I'm not asleep. I'm not even lying down. I'm sitting down and listening. (December 23, 1936)

"*Under the watch*—meaning 시계 아래서—*five towns*—meaning 다섯 개의 동리.[3] This young man loved smoking more than anything in the world—smoked the most fragrant tobacco through a long—curved pipe—and puff—puffing out smoke was his sole happiness."

(I've been needlessly chain-smoking since I got to Tokyo. When rage pops—up— there's no way I can suppress my hysteria unless I inhale the smoke—deep—into my lungs.)

"She had a love affair! His elegant taste—his graceful temperament—the woman declared her love for him in her suicide note—why did she have to die?— Professor Yi—I wouldn't have killed myself if I were her. Is it possible to love some-one to death?—they say it is. But I'm not sure."

(I was a fool from the start. I made a promise to Yŏn that I would die with her. She said she loved me to death, but after paying me a visit at the hospital, within twenty, thirty minutes, she was already in the arms of S, whom I had my suspicions about.)

"However, Professor—I'm very fond of his personality. His smoking is delightful, his voice is delightful—when I read this story it feels as if his voice is—ringing, ringing in my ears. If he asked me to die with him, I can't really say what I'd do till that very moment, but right now, I feel as if I could. Professor, do you think it's possible to really love someone to death? If it is, I want to try falling in love."

(However, dear childish Miss C, Yŏn asked me if we could live instead, after two weeks of promising to die with me. Fooled. I was fooled from that moment on. I foolishly believed we'd live. Not only that. Yŏn even said she loved me.)

"I only read the story up to here—the young man in the end—travels to somewhere—far. To forget about everything."

(This is Tokyo. Why on earth did I come here? I'm poor as a church mouse—*Cocteau* said—Talentless Artists, it's no use flaunting your poverty. Ah—what other talent do I have left besides the talent of pimping my poverty? This is the Kandaku Jinbocho district. When I was younger, I ordered some *hagaki*⁴ cards of the International Modern Art Exhibition that was held here. Now, I'm here, ill.)

"Professor! Do you love the woman in the story?—you do, don't you?—wonderful—think of it as a beautiful death—a man loved that much—would be happy—yes—Professor—Professor, Professor."

(Professor Yi Sang's chin and around his lips—were covered with a thick beard. Grown splendidly.)

"Professor—what—are you thinking about?—hello?—the tobacco's all gone—ah—your pipe might catch fire—open—your eyes, please. I'm done with my story. Hello?—what were you thinking about?"

(Ah—such a beautiful voice. From far away—from outside—so sleek and shiny like a pricey watch—*pianissimo*—am I dreaming? For a whole hour I listened to the voice rather than the *story*. An hour—well it felt like an hour, but it was only ten minutes—did I doze off? I have memorized the entire *story*. I wasn't asleep. It was that flowy, lovely voice that dozed away, gently embracing my sense organs.)

Dream—wish it were a dream. But I wasn't sleeping or lying down.

3

What if your pipe catches fire?

I'll put it out then. But S chuckled—he grinned and began to scold me.

"Sang! Break up with Yŏn. It would be the best thing. Sang and Yŏn as a couple? So contrived that I can't bear to look at you two."

"How so?"

This S guy was, no, Yŏn was S's girl before me. Today, S and I are sitting across from each other, smoking and chatting. Were we ever friends before?

"Sang! I've read your essay 'EPIGRAM.'[5] Yŏn and this 'Yim' in your essay—ha ha—they're one and the same. Sang! I find your two-bit superiority complex hilarious. 'Yim' had a fling just once—ha ha—just once?"

"So what? (I'm so shocked that I could faint.) More than once?—how many times then? S! Spill it! You and Yŏn—how many times?"

"Well, just know that it was more than once."

Dream—wish this was all a dream. But from October 23 to 24,[6] I didn't sleep. I didn't dream.

(Angels—there are no angels anywhere. Because they've all married.)

From the 23, ten at night, I used every trick in the book to torture Yŏn.

On the 24 when the sky lit up—at daybreak, Yŏn finally opened her mouth. Ah! It felt like an eternity!

"The first time—tell me!"

"Some inn at Incheon."

"I already know that. The second time—tell me!"

"......"

"Say it!"

"In S's office at N Building."

"The third time—tell me!"

"......"

"Say it!"

"At Ŭmbyŏkjŏng, outside of the East Gate."

"The fourth time—tell me!"

"......"

"Say it!"

"......"

"Say it!"

In the desk drawer by my bedside, there's a shaving knife, its blade blue. If I slashed her wrist—the bitch would die immediately, spewing blood. However—

I shaved early, clipped my fingernails, changed clothes, and as usual, on October 24, as if my body were already rotting, I was engrossed in my own thoughts as I put my hat on then took it off as if greeting someone, and the room—the smell, where Yŏn and I had slept together for half a year—I looked around at the things we bought for the room, including a goldfish whose dream was also never fulfilled— the autumn was at its peak inside the room, adorned with a single chrysanthemum.

4

However, in Miss C's room—I hear people are already *skating* in my hometown— these two chrysanthemums are so fresh.

Mr. C and Miss C lived in this room. When I referred to Miss C as "wife," she got angry. But when I asked Mr. C, he said Miss C was his wife. I hadn't decided yet what I was in relation to these two, but came to visit them anyway because my life in Tokyo was too lonely.

Under the watch—a *lecture* on 시계 아래서 has ended, but Mr. C kept on smoking through his traditional Korean pipe, and I kept my eyes closed. Miss C's dreamy voice. It had no *intonation*. Flowing endlessly, softly.

I should get going.

"*Sŏnsaengnim* (*Professor?*—what a frightful honorific for an older male.), what's wrong?—don't you like the *kibun*[7] of our room? (*Feel? Kibun* is certainly not a Korean word) Please stay longer—it's not your bedtime yet. Yes? Let's—talk some more."

I stared at Miss C's face as her voice flowed out. Mr. C was as healthy as a tiger, so Miss C was very pale and her lips were practically blue. With her *osage*[8] hairdo, she'll go to school tomorrow. And she'll continue to study *under the watch*.

Having—
no secret is like having no wealth at all, poor and lonely...

The lecturer had no clue why Miss C's lips were so blue besides the fact that she had a mild case of intestinal parasites.

The lecturer blushed at her daring question, then, recalling his superior position, he yelled.

"What would you young ones know—?"

But Yŏn snorted. Why wouldn't we know?—Yŏn was now a sweet twenty, and when she was sixteen, during her free time at high school, she took home economics and gym, and she tore her underwear. Since then, she took these classes only occasionally.

Six—seven—eight—nine—ten.

Five teenage years—in three years, does a dog's tail turn into a sable brush or not—?

Home economics was taught by the school superintendent, a cooking class was taught by Professor Old Maid, and Korean literature was taught by Professor Pock-Faced—.

"Professor, Professor—can you guess what this cute Yŏn did last night?"

The blackboard motto: "A Graceful Virtuous Woman," rearranged to read "A Woman Secretly Steals Virtue."

"Professor, Professor—can you guess why my lips are so blue?"

On the day Yŏn went to meet S at Ŭmbyŏkjŏng, outside the East Gate, she had her English literature class at R University. The night before, she met with me and promised me her love and a future with me, and the next day, in the afternoon, she studied *Gissing* and *Hawthorne*, then that night, she went to East Gate with S and took off her clothes, then the following day, because it was Monday, she went on an outing with me outside of East Gate and we French-kissed. Neither S, nor Professor K, nor I knew what Yŏn did last night. S, Professor K, and I were all idiots, while Yŏn was a genius at this cat-and-mouse game—meow.

Before Yŏn left the N Building, she had to use the WC. Outside it took her another fifteen minutes to make her way through the GO STOP foot traffic at the gate.

"Hey there, hey there, can you guess what Yŏn did inside Mr. S's office, on the second floor?"

Even then Yŏn's skin was glowing like a fresh apple. But poor Professor Yi Sang had no proof at all, he couldn't even get angry about the traffic—he was poorer and even more boring than me, a poor church mouse.

"Miss C! You need to get to bed early since you have class tomorrow." I insisted that I leave. Miss C gave me a flower for my room.

"I heard that your place is pretty bleak."

There wasn't even a vase in my room. I asked for the whiter blossom of the two and pinned it to my left lapel. Then I stepped out.

5

I glanced around—a room without a single chrysanthemum. Well—if all goes as planned, I won't have to see this ugly room ever again—and no wonder I started to tear up—.

Now that I put on my hat I'd just taken off, it seemed that I was all done saying my goodbyes to Yŏn. She followed several steps behind me. But on that ordinary date of October 24, I was more desperate to know how many days it took for a corpse to start rotting.

"Sang! Where're you going?"

I said on an impulse,

"Tokyo."

Of course, I just made that up. But Yŏn didn't stop me. I stepped out.

Well, I was out—where, how, what should I do next?

Before the sun set over the west mountains, I needed to become a corpse and start rotting within two, three days, but how?

My plan was a bit foggy. For the past ten long years—I thought of suicide every time I washed my face. But I had no idea how to commit to it or execute it.

I tried reciting the names of all kinds of trendy and lethal pharmaceuticals.

Then I thought of possible places such as the footbridge, the power station, the rooftop of the Hwashin Mall, and the Kyŏngwŏn railroad.

But then I—thought, really, this kind of list was ridiculous—I couldn't laugh yet. I couldn't laugh. The sun had set. Hurry. I was somewhere on the outskirts of the city. I felt I should get back into the city, regardless. Metropolis—the teeming, teeming, unfamiliar faces of the crowd. The streetlamps were damp with fog. They say London, England, is also like this—.

6

A night market of used books was up and running on Suzuran Street in the Jinbocho district, where NAUKA[9] bookstore was. At the end of the year—Suzuran Street was beautifully decorated. I staggered along the asphalt road, wet with mist, my legs cold and weak from having skipped my dinner. Then I threw away my last twenty cents on a book of everyday English published by the *Times*. Four thousand words—.

Four thousand words is a lot of words. With a foreign language as big as the ocean under my armpit, I couldn't easily become hungry. Oh—I'm full.

Jinta[10]—the *jinta* band was playing a melancholic tune, popular during the Meiji period. The four players—*clarinet*, *cornet*, bass, and snare drum—were hired by a boutique that wanted to make the most of the holiday season. Beyond melodramatic, they made an outlandish street-corner scene. Why? They were young women in bloom! They wore matching pink military outfits, their caps decorated with garish red feathers.

The asphalt was wet. On both sides of Suzuran Street, lily of the valley–shaped lamps were also wet. Even the sound of the clarinet—was soaked—with tears.

And my mind was soaked—with fog.

They say London is like this.

"Yi Sang! What are you dreaming about now?"

A man's voice slapped my shoulder. It was Mr. Y, a law-school grad who thought theatre was more amusing than life. Why? Because life is a nuisance and theatre a bagatelle.

"I went to your place but you weren't there!"

"Sorry."

"Let's go to the *Empress* Café."

"Sounds—good."

In *ADVENTURE IN MANHATTAN Jean Arthur* enjoys a cup of coffee. Mr. Kubo[11] the writer says—add cream to coffee and it smells like rat piss. But I was able to enjoy my coffee as much as *Joel McCrea*—.

MOZART's number 41, "Jupiter Symphony." I discreetly tried to penetrate *Mozart's* magic, but I got very dizzy from hunger.

"Let's go to the Shinjuku district."

"Shinjuku?"

"Let's go to that bar, NOVA."

"Let's go, let's go."

The bar hostess was wearing a *rubashka. Nova* is an *Esperanto* word. A worm kept on gnawing at the heart of a guy wearing a *hunting* cap. Poet Ji-yong![12] Then, Yi Sang is no son of a rich man, he is nothing!

Beer in December was cold, cold. The prison cell is always dark whether day or night—*Gorky*'s sorrowful song "The Wayfarer"—I don't know this song at all.[13]

7

You may be endlessly despondent, day and night. But, Yu-jŏng![14] Don't be sad. You have a higher destiny!

The above motto, glued to the front of his desk, was for Yu-jŏng a sign of being at the crossroads of life and death. He was balancing on a knife-edge. He said that he'd cried, unable to sit or stand, waiting for me to arrive.

"Are you still coughing up blood?"

"Yes—every day is no better or worse."

"Is your hemorrhoid still in a bad way?"

"Yes—every day is no better or worse."

While I was roaming in the fog, I impulsively bought two packs of *Macaw* cigarettes for myself and pears for Yu-jŏng before dropping by. By the time I noticed that he was trying to mask his ghostly appearance with a vase of garish flowers and the smell of disinfectant, I had no energy left to remember why I'd even bothered to come.

"Losing faith is as easy as losing one's health, like being tricked by Death."

"Brother Yi Sang! Have you finally lost faith, only today? Now—finally—today—finally—now."

Yu-jŏng! If you were alright with it, I had planned to carry it out tonight. I don't want to die from something vile. I'd rather kill myself and become an unfortunate genius who died at twenty-seven.

Yu-jŏng and Yi Sang—their splendid, sanctimonious double suicide from a broken heart—I don't know how I'll cope with such a bloated lie.

"However, I intend to lie till the moment of my death, even in my suicide note."

"Look here,"

as Yu-jŏng untied his shirt, his chest was as thin as a straw basket. His emaciated chest rose then crinkled, his last breaths, words were melancholic.

"Hope of tomorrow is overflowing."

Yu-jŏng wept. Because he had forgotten all other expressions except this.

"Brother Yu-jŏng! I'm going to take the first ship to Tokyo."

"....."

"We may not see each other again."

"....."

I inwardly cursed this visit to Yu-jŏng many times as I bid him goodbye. It was late. Yŏn was waiting at my place with a meal prepared for me, winding countless secrets through her fingers. I restrained my hands from slapping her, and used them instead for packing for my departure tomorrow.

Yŏn! She was a genius of meow. I was going to become a genius of misfortune, but couldn't and returned here. Like this, like this! Right?

8

I couldn't bear it any longer, so on a small piece of paper, I jotted a note and handed it to the kid.

"Are you also a genius of meow? By all means, you're a genius. I've lost. The fact that I'm giving in and babbling like an idiot, indicates my defeat."

He wore a Cheil High School badge. HANDSOME BOY—at the strait, two in the morning with a cape on[15]—sat still next to me and held out for an hour (Or more?).

I remained mute as a balloon. I played every trick in the book to make this good-looking genius open his mouth first, but I failed. I lost.

You are thinking of your playful horse. Then, Horse! Galloping horse! Sir, you're graceful, but Sir, why do you look so sad?[16] Why? (This kid's rude.)

"Sad? Ha—of course I'm sad—I'm living in the twentieth century but under the morals of the nineteenth century, so I'm forever limping. I must be sad—even if I'm not—I need to force myself to feel sad—I need to strike a melancholic *pose* at least—want to know why I haven't killed myself? Ha! It's my habit to recommend suicide only to others. I won't kill myself. I act as if I will sometime soon, but I betray everyone's expectations. Oh—but it's no use anymore. Look. My arms. I'm skin and bones. Ha ha. I want to laugh, but I've no muscle. I want to cry, but I've no muscle. I'm a skeleton. Someone erased me—my identity with ink correction fluid. I'm a mere trace—of myself."

Namiko the NOVA *waitress* had the role of a talented *aburae*[17] artist, the kid sister of Kollontai, the daughter of Ibsen's Nora. The artist Miss Namiko and playwright Mr. Y were speaking in French about the world of the fourth dimension.

The rhythm of French was as dreamy as the lecture on *under the watch* by Miss C. I was so overcome with frustration that I started to weep. Tears streamed down my face. Namiko tried to comfort me.

"What are you? Namiko? Last night you were at some *machiai*,[18] sitting on a cushion for fifteen minutes—no, no, you were sitting on a chair with your legs crossed. Tell me—hee hee—was it at Ŭmbyŏkjŏng? At S's office—the second door on the right inside N Building? (Oh—silly Yi Sang. There are no such places in Tokyo.) A girl's face is a *damanegi*.[19] You can keep peeling it off. She will never show her real identity even if there's nothing more left to peel."

One in the morning at Shinjuku—I wanted to have a smoke instead of a love affair.[20]

9

The morning of December 23, at Jinbocho, in my wretched room, I broke out with fever from hunger. I received two letters during a coughing fit.

"If you really love me, please return right away. I stay awake at night waiting for you, Yu-jŏng."

"Please come back as soon as you receive this letter. Your warm room and your beloved Yŏn are waiting for you in Seoul. Yours, Yŏn."

Tonight Miss C gave me a single white chrysanthemum as if to scold my pointless homesickness. But by one in the morning the flower was gone from Yi Sang's lapel as he teetered on the train platform in Shinjuku. Whose boots have stepped on it? But—one *dancer* with an artificial flower pinned to his dark coat. I'm a foreign puppy. What deep-seated secret do you carry in the shadow of your thick makeup?

Having—no secret is like having no wealth at all, poor and lonely! Look at me!

March 1939

1. The title is in Chinese: 失花, meaning "Lost Flower." But phonetically, in Korean, it has multiple meanings: "true story," "accidental fire," "breakup." Yi Sang's play on words introduces an autobiographical story of a failed relationship and his time in Tokyo, where he died. Yi Sang appears in the story as himself, as do a few writer friends from the literary circle he joined, the Circle of Nine. This group, founded in 1933, plays a formal role in that the story is subdivided into nine segments—each like a brief or long cinematic take. This is the only story by Yi Sang that depicts his life in Tokyo. It was published posthumously in the magazine *Munjang* in March of 1939.

2. This line is from Yi Sang's last essay, "Nineteenth Century," published in a journal called *Samsa Munhak* in 1937. In the essay, Yi emphasizes the importance of privacy between couples, but holds that adultery shouldn't be forgiven.

Samsa Munhak featured younger poets and writers who were influenced by surrealism, and they revered Yi Sang's experimental serial poem, "Crow's Eye View." One of the surrealists in the group was Chu Yŏng-sŏp, a playwright. Chu, as a foreign student, was involved in avant-garde theater in Tokyo while Yi Sang was there. Mr. C, a lover or husband of Miss C, is believed to be modeled after Chu.

3. "*Under the watch*—meaning 시계 아래서—*five towns*—meaning 다섯 개의 동리." The italicized phrases indicate Korean transliterations of English words. The Korean script indicates where Yi Sang translates the foreign words into Korean within the same sentence. "Five towns" is in reference to Arnold Bennett's novel *Anna of the Five Towns*, a story of a love triangle, first published in 1902. Throughout our translation, we have used italics to indicate Yi Sang's transliteration of foreign words from English, Japanese, and French. We have used fully capitalized English words to indicate words appearing in English in Yi Sang's original text.

4. *hagaki*: the Japanese word for "postcard."

5. "EPIGRAM" is the title of an essay by Yi Sang, published in a mainstream journal called *Yŏsŏng* (Woman), 1936. The essay is about his new marriage and his upcoming trip to Tokyo. "Yim" in the essay refers to Pyŏn Tong-nim, the woman he married in the summer of 1936.

6. October 23 refers to the date when Yŏn and Yi Sang married.

7. *kibun*: meaning "feel" or "mood," is used both in Korean and Japanese.

8. *osage*: the Japanese word for "braided pig-tails."

(Drawing by Don Mee Choi)

9. NAUKA: a bookstore specializing in Russian books. It's still in operation in Jinbocho 1–34.

10. *Jinta* refers to Western-style music played by a brass street-band, often hired to advertise goods.

11. Mr. Kubo is the protagonist of an autobiographical story of a flâneur, *A Day in the Life of Writer Mr. Kubo*, by modernist Pak T'ae-wŏn (1909–86). Kubo was also his pen name. Yi Sang drew illustrations for the story when the novel was serialized in *Chosun Chungang Daily*, 1934. Pak became a member of the Circle of Nine in 1933. In 1950, soon after the Korean War began, he crossed to North Korea with several notable authors, leaving his children and wife behind. He continued to write and publish in North Korea.

12. Poet Ji-yong is Chŏng Ji-yong (1902–50), considered one of the most important early modern poets of Korea. He was also a translator from the English and belonged to the Circle of Nine. "... gnawing at the heart of a guy" and "Yi Sang is no son of a rich man, he is nothing!" are in reference to Chŏng Ji-yong's poem *Café France*," first published in the literary journal *Hakjo*, in 1926. *Hakjo* was run by Korean students in Japan.

CAFÉ FRANCE

Beneath the transplanted palm tree
a tilted lamp.
Let's go to *Café France*.

This guy's wearing a *rubaska*.
The other guy a *bohemian necktie*.
The skinny guy takes the lead.
The night rain's as thin as a snake's eyes
but light weeps on the *pavement*.
Let's go to *Café France*.

This guy's head's a red apple, still a little green.
The other guy's heart's a worm-infested rose.
The rain-drenched guy takes off like a swallow.

"*Oh, oh, parrot* husband! *Good evening*!"

"*Good evening*!" (How are you my friend?)

A tulip girl snoozes
under the sloped *curtain*!

I'm no rich man's son, I'm nothing.
My pale palms stand out, making me sad!
I have no country, no house.
My sad cheeks against the marble *table*!

Oh, oh, foreign puppy
lick my feet,
lick my feet.

(Translated by Don Mee Choi and Joyelle McSweeney.)

13. Maxim Gorky's play *The Lower Depth*, retitled in Korean as *A Night's Lodging*, opened in Korea in 1934. Chu Yŏng-sŏp the playwright had performed in the play.

14. Yu-jŏng is the novelist Kim Yu-jŏng (1908–37). He was one of the writers of the Circle of Nine. He participated in a rural literacy movement during the early 1930s. He often wrote about the fate of poor, displaced women in the rural areas. He died of TB just before Yi Sang, in the same year.

15. "At the strait, two in the morning with a cape on" is in reference to Chŏng Ji-yong's poem "The Strait" (1935). The strait in the poem refers to the Korea Strait, a passage between Korea and Japan.

THE STRAIT

The horizon swells up to the eyelashes, peeping through the eye of a jetty as if made by a cannonball,

the sky sinks and
broods like a large, mean hen.

My place is
where the transparent bottom-fish march!

My ears above the collar of my cape are like shells,
filled with the horn blowing from the deserted island—

and the loneliness of the strait at two in the morning
    wears a halo of light.
Like a girl, I cry without tears

My youth is my country!
The clear skies of the port of tomorrow!

The sea route intensifies like true love.
Now the midnight sun glows.

(Translated by Don Mee Choi and Joyelle McSweeney.)

16. "Horse! Galloping horse! Sir, you're graceful, but Sir, why do you look so sad?" are lines in reference to Chŏng Ji-yong's poem "Horse" (1927).

HORSE

Horse, galloping horse,
You're graceful
But why do you look so sad?

Horse, you live amongst people,
I feed you black and green beans.

The horse doesn't know who its parents are
At night, it falls asleep looking at the faraway moon

(Translated by Don Mee Choi and Joyelle McSweeney.)

17. *aburae*: Japanese word for "oil painting."

18. *machiai*: Japanese word for "meeting place," "a teahouse."

19. *damanegi*: Japanese word for "onion." Contemporary South Korean poet Kim Hyesoon has a poem, "Onion," that echoes Yi Sang's sentiment:

ONION

Under the faucet a man peeled a woman's skin
The woman cacklecackled and peeled easily like an
    onion
As a layer of dark night peeled off transparent day
    soared
Blood draindrained down a pipe
like the mushy inside of a fresh egg
Someone cried, stopitstopit why are you all acting this
    way?
When day gets suckled the sadtastingspicytasting
    night soars
Day and night kept this up for a thousand ten
    thousand years, for all eternity
yet the woman peeled layerafterlayer

The man who peeled an onion cried because of its
    sap
and the woman cried along with him
ah andsoregardless today's day left and night arrived
yet I didn't know where I was
maybe I was hidden somewhere between the spicy
    layers
so when I kept asking where I was and turned around
the woman's body was just as before
and the man kept crying and crying and peeled the
    woman's skin
After I was all peeled like an onion, I wasn't there
    anymore
but the I that used to call me I was hiding somewhere
Night hid and trembled under the wood floor after
    taking off its spicy skin
yet the sea endlessly took off and put on a pair of
    pants
and yet it was hotinsummer and coldinwinter and
    everything drifted away
Isn'tthisthemostbeautifulstoryintheworld?

(From *All the Garbage of the World, Unite!* [2011] translated by Don Mee Choi.)

20. "I wanted to have a smoke instead of a love affair" is in reference to the last stanza of Chŏng Ji-yong's poem "The Strait, Again."

On my first sea journey at twenty-one
I learned how to smoke before a love affair.

FOLLOWING: **Don Mee Choi, *Yi Sang's Attic*. Collage from photocopied pages of Yi Sang's poems, with her father's notes.**

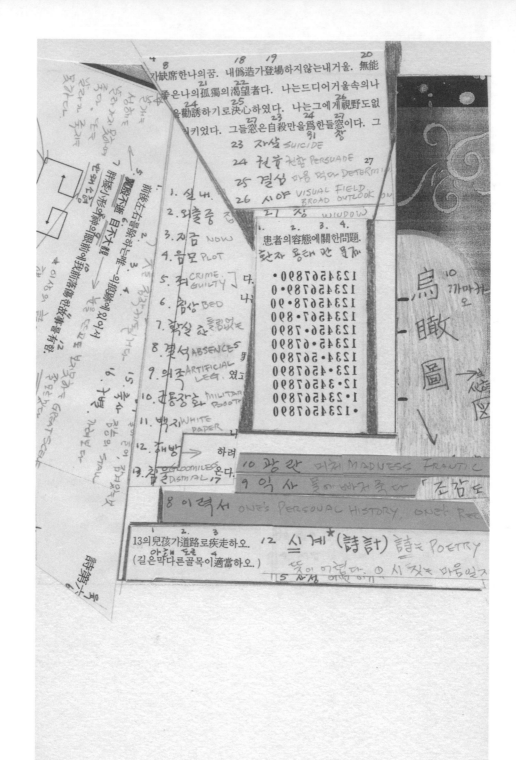

Afterword: Thirteen for Yi Sang, for Arachne

JOYELLE MCSWEENEY

1 I caught Yi Sang like a disease. I caught Yi Sang not from a text but from an image: an artwork by Fi Jae Lee, *The Poet Yi Sang's Wedding and Funeral*. In this double sculpture, the "poet" is manikin-sized, sculpted from wire, paper, lace, and fish skin; his wife is an oversized wire dress form, larger than her husband, sculpted from what looks like clothes hangers. She is bridal white and, in the way of the arachnid world, larger than her husband. The wedding is a funeral because to mate is to be eaten, to become absorbed in the dark matter of the lover's body. Eros is Thanatos because they're made of the same stuff: innards, formal attire, a folie à deux, a mis en abyme.

2 Spider&Spider in their spider-hole. Spider&Spider&Spider&Spider&

3 Delicate and rotting like fish skin, the male spider tells the changes of the season from his wife's socks. He tumbles into her image, and the room ingests both of them before spitting him out in the street and towards eventfulness. In Yi Sang's narratives, events are what happen outside the spider-hole. A hole at the center of every plot. A hole shaped like Yi Sang. A hole named Yi Sang.

4 To be a hole and a spider, to lie in one's bed as on one's bier, to be outside of history, to refuse the historical imperatives of empire, of the occupier, of the patriarchy. This is decadence as resistance, a refusal to compete in survival of the fittest.

While Yi Sang's protagonists *prefer not to* beg, bow, circumstances force this subservience. Yet there is an erotic gain to this activity when reenacted in the spider-hole, a luxury in penury, a revaluation not according to the hierarchies of the occupation.

5 In this sense, Yi Sang's body of work is the spider-hole, a place where values are reversed and upended, where proscriptions are resisted, where a sex-worker bride dominates the prone man, where the forcefulness of masculinity is shed like an exoskeleton, where the powerless explore the subaltern zone of their stigmatized embodiment.

6 I caught Yi Sang from an image; next, I read a translation of "Flowering Tree"; next, I read multiple translations of flowering tree, in which the tree catches art from a tree:

FLOWERING TREE

On an open field   a flowering tree stands   with no other like it   nearby   the flowering tree blossoms with a burning heart   as if thinking of   another flowering tree   burns its heart.   The flowering tree cannot reach the tree flowering in its thoughts   I wildly fled   for the sake of   one flowering tree   I truly did such weird mimicry.

Art's erotic likenesses. The immobility of the tree is radiant; the tree is as much flaring as flowering and it drives the speaker to Art. While the speaker flees into the endless mimicry of Art, the "weird mimicry," rare replications, the ultimate place, the mise en abyme, one guesses that he, too, is radiantly immobilized in fire like the tree.

7 To be annealed in mimicry. The purity of artifice. Personhood as persona. The labyrinthine shape of a spiderweb. The permeable mirror. The web of likenesses.

8 If this body of work is a mise en abyme, mirror upon mirror, with Yi Sang's alter egos performing pageants of inertness, inept gesture, and refusal to succeed despite evident talent, Yi Sang himself was more like the modernist icon of the dynamo, nervy and mobile, his illustrations, poetry, and prose appearing in the most improbable of venues, from popular newspapers to bureaucratic bulletins, under the nose of the bourgeois and the occupying regime alike, his impossible cafés opening and closing, his debts opening and closing like gills. Reversal, imprintation, replication, proliferation, the very techniques of the printing press, were also the techniques of propagating an avant-garde against the enforced conservatism of both patriarchal structure and the occupying regime. These were survival strategies Yi Sang, foster child and governmental clerk, knew in his bones. These are also the survival strategies of *Mycobacterium tuberculosis*, the bacterium that killed Yi Sang at 27 after a stint in a Japanese labor camp for thoughtcrime.

*

9 "O I didn't know there were such revolting holes!" —Kim Hyesoon

10 "The silence of death is the worst kind of silence ... the silence of death cuts the edge off what could have been and never will be, that which we will never know. We'll never know if Buchner would have been bigger than Goethe. I think so, but we'll never know. We'll never know what he might have written at age thirty. And that extends across the whole planet like a stain, an atrocious illness that in one way or another puts our habits in check, our most ingrained certainties." —Roberto Bolaño

11

*

12 So much that I know about translation I have learned from the working relationship of Don Mee Choi and Kim Hyesoon, of whom Kim Hyesoon has written, "It is like someone who is very much like me." To translate is to enter a web of likenesses and unlikeness, the uncertain, proliferating zone of the text. So it has been a thrilling adventure to join hands with Don Mee Choi and peer with her into the mirror of Yi Sang, sisterly and nonidentical, to become Spider&Spider&Spider&— such weird mimicry.

13 While we were finalizing our texts my baby girl was born and died. Her name was Arachne. She lived thirteen lucky days. After she died, I questioned everything, including whether it was wise to name a baby after an artist who defied the gods. Spider&Spider&. My thoughts ampersand and scatter. They no longer run in a straight line down the alleys. I look sidelong at mirrors and I look for clues in broken glass. *Where is my baby?*

Arachne&Persephone&Eurydice. Arachne, like Ariadne, might drag a dangling string behind her like wet starlight, a cord, a hem, a thread, or a clew as she slips through the channels of the mise en abyme, the mirror, the labyrinth at Marienbad. *The flowering tree cannot reach the tree flowering in its thoughts.* When seen from above, her trail looks like the cosmos, like a glittering web.

TRANSLATORS WHOSE WORK IS CITED: #6: Jack Jung; #9: Don Mee Choi; #10: Natasha Wimmer.

Acknowledgments

The translation of Yi Sang's Korean poetry and prose in this volume was supported by a generous grant from the Literature Translation Institute of Korea (LTI Korea). I am indebted to the editors and staff of Wave Books for their invaluable help in putting this volume together. Thank you to Joshua Beckman for accepting this project without any hesitation.

Thank you to fellow literary translators for their interest and excitement for this project. To the Korean literary translators collective Smoking Tigers for their brilliant creative energy and camaraderie. To Bruce Fulton and David McCann for introducing me to the community of Korean literary translators. To Deborah Smith for her insightful notes. To Aron Aji, Derick Mattern, Bruna Dantas Lobato, Jianan Qian, Yvonne Cha, Stella Wong, and many other members of University of Iowa's literary community for their encouragements and advice on the drafts of these translations. My love to Anna Polonyi and Carole Cassier for taking care of me during the endless revisions of this manuscript. To Emily Jungmin Yoon for her friendship and work as a fellow Yi Sang translator.

I am thankful to Professor Kwon Youngmin of Seoul National University (SNU), whose scholarship on Yi Sang literature has been an important guide in this project. Thank you to the friends and colleagues at SNU for their help in navigating and tracking down original Yi Sang texts. My love goes to Yoon Kuk-Hee of SNU—my sister, confidant, and fellow scholar of modern Korean literature.

Thank you to the editors of the journals and magazines in which some of the poems have previously appeared. To Sasha Dugdale of *Modern Poetry in Translation* for her interest and faith in Yi Sang's poems. To Young-Jun Lee of *Azalea: Journal of Korean Literature and Culture* for his brilliant work in introducing and supporting translations of old and new Korean literature.

I am thankful also to my mentors in English poetry for their continued support. To Jorie Graham, for your incredible gift of love of poetry and who first suggested I should translate Korean poetry. To Lucie Brock-Broido, for challenging me to be a better poet with her friendship and teaching.

To James Simpson, for the years of believing in my ability. To Mark Levine, for his demanding guidance that keeps pressure on my writing.

My deepest gratitude goes to Don Mee Choi for discovering my Yi Sang translations and believing in me through these years. Your editorial work for this volume is truly inspiring, and I have become a better writer and translator with your help. I am grateful again to Joshua Beckman for his close reading and editorial suggestions. Thank you to fellow translators of Yi Sang in this volume, Joyelle McSweeney and Sawako Nakayasu, for their amazing work. I am humbled to be in your company.

These translations of Yi Sang began over a decade ago in a college dorm in snowy New England. To my brother Rob Mrkonich, you have been there with me from the beginning; thank you for reading these translations since their infancy. Thank you to Sophie Duvernoy and Becky Fradkin for their constant friendship in life and literature. And to my mother, Susan Myoungsook Jung: you started this journey for me by showing me poems of Yi Sang for the first time. Without you, nothing would be possible.

JACK JUNG

*

I have long admired Yi Sang's poetry, ever since the Zainichi Korean poet Kyongmi Park asked me to translate his "Poem No. 1" from the "Crow's Eye View" series, to be featured on a big, beautiful poster called *artictoc,* a publication of the Yotsuya Art Studium. Over these years, I have also worked with my co-editor Eric Selland on an anthology of 20th century Japanese poetry, debating whether we would include the poems Yi Sang wrote in Japanese. His colonial relationship to the Japanese language makes the question difficult to answer. What would Yi Sang himself have wanted? My own Japanese heritage has made me hesitant to decide on his behalf, which is why I am all the more pleased to share my translations first in this carefully considered project. My enormous gratitude, fondness, and admiration for Don Mee Choi, for her fearless work and deep kindness.

Many thanks also to Jack Jung and Joyelle McSweeney for their tremendous work. To Joshua Beckman, Heidi Broadhead, Blyss Ervin, and the entire team at Wave. To Kyongmi Park and Kenjiro

Okazaki (for architectural expertise as well), to Will Gardner, Toshiko Ellis, Walter K. Lew, Samuel Perry, Janet Poole, Eric Selland, Alys Moody for their scholarship, and also to Erica Hunt, Susan Bernofsky, Gabrielle Civil, Hitomi Yoshio, Corey Wakeling, Taylor Mignon, Jordan Smith. Big deep thanks to John Granger, always. With love to my family in Japan, to Eugene Kang, and to Marina and Jona, who love to read.

Gratitude to the following editors of publications where some of these translations were first published or are forthcoming: *The Colorado Review*, *The Iowa Review*, *Peripheries*, and *Poetry*.

SAWAKO NAKAYASU

*

My deepest gratitude to Joshua Beckman with whom I have brainstormed and edited from the very beginning of this project. To Wave Books for welcoming Yi Sang. Thank you, Blyss Ervin, Heidi Broadhead, and Catherine Bresner. To LTI of Korea for their continuous support. To Kim Hyesoon for sending me *Yi Sang Munhak Taesajŏn* (2017) by Kwon Youngmin. To Walter K. Lew, who has previously established Yi Sang's visibility in the US through his brilliant translations. To wonderful fellow poets and translators Jack, Sawako, and Joyelle.

"Yi Sang's House" with the collage appeared in *Harriet,* for the Poetry Foundation, April 2020.

An excerpt of "Spider&SpiderMeetPigs" appeared in *North American Review,* 303.1, Winter 2018.

DON MEE CHOI

*

I am grateful to Don Mee, Jack, Sawako, and Wave Books for involvement in this project, to LTI Korea for supporting my continuing education in Korean literature and for the chance to interact with Korean writers and critics, and to Fi Jae Lee and Walter K. Lew for introducing me to Yi Sang.

JOYELLE MCSWEENEY

Biographical Notes

JACK SAEBYOK JUNG is a graduate of Iowa Writers' Workshop where he was a Truman Capote Fellow. He was born in Seoul, South Korea, and immigrated to the United States. He received his BA in English from Harvard and MA in Korean language and literature from Seoul National University. He currently spends his time between Iowa City and Cambridge, Massachusetts.

SAWAKO NAKAYASU is an artist working with language, performance, and translation—separately and in various combinations. She has lived mostly in the US and Japan, briefly in France and China, and translates from Japanese. Her books include *Some Girls Walk Into The Country They Are From* (forthcoming, Wave Books), *Pink Waves* (forthcoming, Omni-dawn), *The Ants* (Les Figues Press), and the translation of *The Collected Poems of Chika Sagawa* (forthcoming, Modern Library), as well as *Mouth: Eats Color—Sagawa Chika Translations, Anti-Translations, & Originals* (reprint forthcoming, Wave Books), a multilingual work of both original and translated poetry. She is co-editor, with Eric Selland, of an anthology of 20th Century Japanese Poetry (forthcoming, New Directions). She teaches at Brown University.

Born in Seoul, South Korea, DON MEE CHOI is the author of *DMZ Colony*, *Hardly War*, *The Morning News Is Exciting* and several chapbooks and pamphlets of poems and essays. She has received a Whiting Award, Lannan Literary Fellowship, Lucien Stryk Translation Prize, and DAAD Artists-in-Berlin Fellowship. She has translated several collections of Kim Hyesoon's poetry, including *Autobiography of Death*, which receieved the 2019 International Griffin Poetry Prize.

JOYELLE MCSWEENEY is the author of ten books of poetry, stories, novels, essays, translations and plays, including the poetry double volume *Toxicon and Arachne* (Nightboat Books) and *The Necropastoral: Poetry, Media, Occults*, a work of decadent ecopoetics. With

Johannes Göransson, she co-edits the international press Action Books, publishing such authors as Raúl Zurita, Hiromi Ito, Josué Guébo, Choi Seungja and Kim Hyesoon, while supporting translators like Daniel Borzutzky, Don Mee Choi, Katherine Hedeen, Katrine Øgaard Jensen, Michelle Gil-Montero, Jeffrey Angles, and many others. She is proud to serve as the 2020 mentor for ALTA's Emerging Translators Mentorship Program in Korean poetry. She teaches at Notre Dame.